Wordplay

Arranged and Deranged Wit

⅋

D1564573

OTHER BOOKS
BY HOWARD RICHLER

*How Happy Became Homosexual and
Other Mysterious Semantic Shifts* (2013)

*Strange Bedfellows: The Private
Lives of Words* (2010)

Can I Have a Word with You? (2007)

*Global Mother Tongue: The Eight
Flavours of English* (2006)

*A Bawdy Language: How a Second-Rate Language
Slept Its Way to the Top* (1999)

*Take My Words:
A Wordaholic's Guide to the
English Language* (1996)

The Dead Sea Scroll Palindromes (1995)

Wordplay
Arranged and Deranged Wit

Howard Richler

RONSDALE PRESS

RONSDALE PRESS
3350 West 21st Avenue
Vancouver, B.C. Canada V6S 1G7
www.ronsdalepress.com

Typesetting: Julie Cochrane, in Granjon 11.5 pt on 15
Cover Design: David Drummond
Copy Editor: Meagan Dyer
Paper: Ancient Forest Friendly 50lb Resolute Alternative Book Cream FSC
    Recycled — 100% post-consumer waste, totally chlorine-free and acid-free.

Ronsdale Press wishes to thank the following for their support of its publishing program: the Canada Council for the Arts, the Government of Canada through the Canada Book Fund, the British Columbia Arts Council, and the Province of British Columbia through the British Columbia Book Publishing Tax Credit program.

Library and Archives Canada Cataloguing in Publication

Richler, Howard, 1948–, author
    Wordplay: arranged and deranged wit / Howard Richler.

Issued in print and electronic formats.
ISBN 978-1-55380-452-9 (print)
ISBN 978-1-55380-453-6 (ebook) / ISBN 978-1-55380-454-3 (pdf)

    1. English language — Etymology. 2. English language — History.
3. Wit and humor.   I. Title.

PE1574.R53 2016   422   C2015-906707-3   C2015-906722-7

At Ronsdale Press we are committed to protecting the environment. To this end we are working with Canopy and printers to phase out our use of paper produced from ancient forests. This book is one step towards that goal.

Printed in Canada by Marquis Book Printing, Quebec

To Judah & Maya
and in loving memory
of Molly

ACKNOWLEDGEMENTS

Special thanks to Carol Broderick for her work on *Wordplay*. Without her input, this publication would not be the book it is.

Thanks also to Leslie Bank Satz who adds a visual aspect to the book by way of her humorous illustrations. Finally, I must thank my publisher Ron Hatch for his usual understated yet firm suggestions.

Contents

PART II: Deranged Wit

Wordplay

Arranged and Deranged Wit

&

Introduction

NOTWITHSTANDING THE millions of dog and cat owners who (like me) robotically scoop poop and change litter, some misguided souls regard our species as the dominant one on the planet. I suppose this delusion is based on our ability to employ language, allowing us to communicate far more efficiently than other animals. We thus control the planet and, perhaps, will eventually destroy it. Language, however, also performs a far less "serious" purpose.

I'm referring to the propensity of *Homo sapiens* for language play. Most people cavort with their mother tongues, revelling in the sounds and their various meanings. Because language serves a recreational purpose, many people also often "re-create" words for their amusement. John Crosbie, who founded the International Save the Pun Foundation in 1978, succinctly expressed the process of manipulating language when he said, "Puns are their own rewords." The proclivity to pun is hardly an elitist process. Walter Redfern, in his book *Puns*, tells us that "Punning is a free-for-all available to everyone. . . . It is the stock-in-trade of the low comedian and the most sophisticated wordsmith." Redfern adds that puns appeal particularly to people of a "certain temperament." It is my hypothesis that the *inability* to play with language, in one form or another, may augur some form of pathology (or, at the very least, a proclivity to believe that Adam and Eve lived in an exotic garden replete with dinosaurs).

I will admit that pronouncing definitively on what constitutes true wit is a subjective endeavour. Complicating matters even further is the fact that the employment of language wit occurs not only wittingly, but also unwittingly and sometimes even half-wittedly. When we manipulate language for the purpose of wit, I designate this process *arranged wit*. At times, however, humour comes from mistakes that one has made when it appears that we are dealing more with a twit or a nitwit than with a wit. This form I designate *deranged wit*. Ergo, I am making the case that language that is not *arranged* is thus *deranged*.

But how is this manipulation of our language achieved? The arrangement and "derangement" of words in English is facilitated by the multiplicity of meanings many words enjoy. For example, much wordplay treats homonyms as if they were synonyms, as in *Romeo and Juliet* when Romeo asks for a torch and says, "Being but heavy I will bear the light." The flexibility of English aids greatly in this process. A case in point is the fact that over 20 percent of verbs started out their lives as nouns. If you take a gander at your body, you will find that virtually every part, formerly only a noun, has been adapted as a verb, so that from head to toe you can head a committee, face the music, knuckle under, foot the bill, and toe the line.

Also, starting in the twelfth century, the English language underwent a process that eliminated so many declensions and conjugations as well as precise syntax locutions that sometimes it seems that virtually any word can be interpreted in many ways, and often lewdly. For this reason, the verbs "come," "do," "fix," "have," "know," "make" and "put" are all replete with sexual innuendo. These factors contribute to a greater propensity for wordplay in English than in many other languages that are more highly inflected.

Schadenfreude aside, even the kind-hearted enjoy hearing people mangle language. We even revel when they pretend to commit some language screw-up. In fact, the difference between a pun and a fabricated screw-up is not always apparent. Hence, the distinction between *arranged* and *deranged* wit is often murky. Sometimes one pretends that language has been mangled when the reality is that the process of the "mistake" is rather deliberate, and quite cleverly constructed. Such is the case of spoonerisms, which we will consider in Part I, Chapter 2.

Also, many a pun is without wit either because it has been used ad nauseam or is not inherently funny, but here again subjectivity raises its ugly head. We can find some patterns that show how it is that a particular group of people like a particular joke, but to a large extent the process is an individual one affected by a host of factors such as education, gender and class level. Like many other people, I have enjoyed a belly laugh from a text being so badly written that it is riotously amusing. Students in particular often commit mistakes that are rather hilarious. (See malaprops in Part II, Chapter 1.)

In *Wordplay* I have included many of the wittiest examples of language play from known punsters and literary greats. I have also injected much in the way of my own play on words in the form of word definitions (occasionally pictorial) as well as a bevy of new types of word puzzles to delight the reader and to make reading this book and the process of wordplay, in general, a collaborative effort.

Please note that throughout *Wordplay* I use the terms wit and humour interchangeably. Although these words originally had distinct senses ("humour" referred to one's general condition whereas "wit" referred to one's mental capacity), by the seventeenth and eighteenth centuries they became synonymous — unless their senses were being parsed by arcane philosophers. Nowadays, the distinction between them is so blurred that most people would regard it as pedantic to assign them to totally distinct categories. This being said, the eighth definition of "wit" in the *Oxford English Dictionary* (henceforth, *OED*) sums up the sublimity that I associate with witmanship: "That quality of speech or writing which consists in the apt association of thought and expression calculated to surprise and delight by its unexpectedness; later always with the reference to the utterance of brilliant or sparkling things in an amusing way."

I have avoided discussing humour whose intent is the degrading of a particular group because of some supposed deficiency the group possesses. Humiliation is no laughing matter, particularly when one is the nail rather than the hammer. I realize, however, that what is deemed offensive is highly personal, and if any of the wit displayed in the following pages offends someone, I am truly sorry.

And because Shakespeare informs us in *Hamlet* that "Brevity is the soul of wit," I will keep my analysis throughout to a minimum.

Enjoy!

PART I

Arranged Wit

ℊ

"The tongues of mocking wenches are as keen as
is the razor's edge invisible."
— William Shakespeare, *Love's Labour's Lost*

"When I am dead, I hope it may be said: 'His sins were
scarlet, but his books were read.'"
— Hillaire Belloc

"True wit is Nature to advantage dressed,
What oft was thought, but ne'er so well expressed."
— Alexander Pope, *An Essay on Criticism*

⅊

CHAPTER 1

Puns

"In the beginning was the pun."
— Samuel Beckett, *Murphy*

⅊ TO PUN OR NOT TO PUN?

If you are a reticent punster, steel your courage and silence not your tongue, for according to linguist David Crystal in *Language Play* almost "two-thirds of the jokes in a typical language collection rely on puns." The humour in language is often deliberate, but many have posed this ludic question: To pun or not to pun? Puns have been much maligned by a host of commentators. Freud described puns as "cheap," and Oliver Wendell Holmes assailed them as "verbicide." Many writers in seventeenth- and eighteenth-century England, such as John Dryden, Daniel Defoe and Joseph Addison, believed that the English language had approached perfection and that the inherent ambiguity in puns created confusion and impoliteness. In an article in the *Tatler* in 1710, however, Jonathan Swift mocked this "affectation of politeness," because he realized, as Shakespeare did, that individual words possess multiple interpretative possibilities and humour is unavoidable. Puns have had other defenders. Three hundred years ago, Henry Erskine countered the statement that "a pun is the lowest form of wit" by adding that "it is therefore the foundation of all wit," and Oscar Levant opined that it is the "lowest form of humor — when you didn't think of it first."

Charles Lamb connected puns to good humour, when he commented: "I never knew an enemy of puns who was not an ill-natured man. A pun is a noble thing per se; it fills the mind. It is perfect as a sonnet. May my last breath be drawn through a pipe and exhaled as a pun." And James Boswell, who delighted in good company, confided, "A good pun may be admitted among the small excellences of lively conversation."

Punning has, indeed, been a language fixture through the ages. In Homer's *Odyssey*, Odysseus introduces himself to the Cyclops, as Outis, which means "no man" in Greek. When he attacks the giant to escape from the cave, the giant calls for reinforcement from his fellow monsters with the plea "No man is killing me!" Naturally, no one rushes to his aid, proving that the pun is indeed mightier than the sword. Cicero was another habitual grave punster. When a man plowed up the burial ground of his father, Cicero couldn't resist interjecting: "This is truly to cultivate a father's memory."

In the Bible there are many names that could be taken as puns. In Hebrew, *adamah* means ground and *edom* means red. The name Adam may derive from the red earth whence he came. Redman. The name Jacob is derived from the Hebrew word for heel (*ah'kev*), because he held onto the heel of his older twin brother Esau at birth. However, I award Jesus the prize for best Biblical pun. We read in Matthew 16:18: "Thou art Peter (Greek *Petros*), and upon this rock (Greek *petra*) I will build my Church." Upon meeting children from England in the slave market at Rome approximately a millennium and a half ago, and being told they were Anglo-Saxons, Pope Gregory I, guardian of the Rock, punned that the English slaves were *Non Angli, sed angeli*: "not Angles, but angels."

Much later, the heyday of English language puns was the Elizabethan era. This type of wordplay was enjoyed by all strata of society, and people differentiated among all sorts of wordplay, such as "pun," "quibble," "clinch" (or "clench"), "repartee," and "double entendre." Many wordsmiths adhered to a rigid separation among these terms. For example, according to the *OED*, a pun refers to "the use of a word in such a way as to suggest two or more meanings or different associations, or the use of two or more words of the same or nearly the same sound with different meanings, so as to produce a humorous effect; a play on words." A quibble, the *OED* informs us, is "an equivocation, evasion of the point at issue; an argument depending on some likeness or difference between words or their meanings, or on some circumstance of no real importance." If the quibble was considered weak, it would be called a quarterquibble. A carriwitchet, according to the *OED*, designates "a pun, quibble; a hoaxing question or conundrum," whereas a clinch represents "a sharp repartee that twists or turns about the meaning of a word." The *OED* defines the term "double entendre" as "a double meaning; a word or phrase having a double sense, esp., as used to convey an indelicate meaning." It is usually reserved for puns with sexual content such as this ditty: Did you hear about the sleepy bride who couldn't stay awake for a second?

The creation of Elizabethan puns was facilitated by the many recent borrowings from the Romance languages in the thirteenth and fourteenth centuries. Also, the revolutionary changes in English pronunciation at the beginning of the fifteenth century created many new homonyms, the building blocks of puns. Queen Elizabeth I herself puns doubly when she declares, "You may be burly, my Lord of Burleigh, but ye shall make less stir in my realm than the Lord of Leicester."

❧ ORIGIN OF THE WORD "PUN"

We find the first *OED* citation of the word "pun" in John Dryden's 1663 play *The Wild Gallant*, when the character Failer says: "A bare Clinch will serve the turn; a Carwichet, a Quarterquibble, or a Punn." The word itself derives from the Italian *puntiglio*, which means "a fine point," hence a verbal quibble, and is most likely the source of the English "punctilious," which means showing great attention to detail and "correct" behaviour. The term "pundigrion" was also used in the seventeenth century as another form of "pun," but by the early nineteenth century this term was obsolete.

✽ TYPOLOGY OF PUNS

Puns can be divided into a discrete number of categories. First we have
homophonic puns that treat words that are homonyms as synonyms:

> Why is it so wet in London? Because so many kings and
> queens reign there.

Another form is the *homographic pun* which uses words that are spelled
the same but possess different meanings and sounds:

> Did you hear about the optician who fell into a lens grinder
> and made a spectacle of himself?

These two forms can be combined and, when this is done, it is usually
referred to as a *homonymic pun*:

> She was only a rancher's daughter, but all the
> horsemen knew her.

Still another genre is the *compound pun* in which a word or string of
words forms another word or string of words:

> Where do you find giant snails? On the end of
> giants' fingers.

The final type is the *recursive pun* where the second part of the pun
depends on understanding the first part:

> A Freudian slip is where you say one thing and
> mean your mother.

Here the word "mother" has replaced "another," the humour relying on
the listener recognizing Freud's emphasis on the child and adult's relationship with the mother.

✽ SHAKESPEARE'S PUNS

'Tis said that in the art of punning, Shakespeare was great shakes and
without peer. Not everyone, however, appreciated the Bard's puns. Lexi-

Why is it so wet in London?
Because so many kings and queens reign there.

cographer Samuel Johnson said that "a quibble was to Shakespeare his fatal Cleopatra for which he lost the world and was content to do so." In his *A Dictionary of the English Language* (1755), Johnson defines "quibble" as "a low conceit depending on the sound of words." A "punster" is rendered as "a low wit who endeavours at reputation by double meaning." Hardly high praise.

Twentieth-century literary critic William Empson was even harsher. He felt Shakespeare's punnery showed "lack of decision and will-power, a feminine pleasure in yielding to the mesmerism of language, in getting one's way, if at all, by deceit and flattery, for a poet to be so fearfully susceptible to puns." He went on to say, "Many of us could wish the Bard had been more manly in his literary habits." Empson was reiterating a point made by eighteenth-century writer Joseph Addison who believed that puns had to be strictly differentiated from the "manly strokes" of wit and satire. Samuel Taylor Coleridge, on the other hand, was much more understanding of Shakespeare's penchant to pun and stated that "a pun, if congruous with the feeling of a scene is not only allowable . . . but oftentimes the most effective intensive of passions." Clearly, Coleridge understood that the feminine, if such it were, could also be passionately in love with the pun.

One study uncovered some three thousand puns in the Bard's works, with an average of seventy-eight puns per play. Many of these occur at climactic moments. In *Macbeth*, after Macbeth has killed the King, Lady Macbeth displays a lucid dispassion in her use of sound when she avers, "I'll *gild* the faces of the grooms withal. For it must seem their *guilt*." At the beginning of *Julius Caesar*, the cobbler says of shoes that he is a "mender of bad soles," and if they are in danger, he "recovers them" — playing on "soles" and "souls." In *Romeo and Juliet*, the dying Mercutio exits stage left with this vaudevillian pun: "Ask for me tomorrow and you shall find me a grave man." This is but one of the estimated 175 puns in *Romeo and Juliet*. Even the great Dane himself, Hamlet, doggedly can't forgo expiring without the pun "the rest is silence," proving the maxim that "Dying is easy, comedy is hard."

Nowadays, we look at puns as merely exercises in jocularity, but we must bear in mind that in Shakespeare's era, there were few unsuitable moments for puns. Even religious puns were acceptable, as when Romeo says to Juliet:

> O, then, dear saint, let lips do what hands do.
> They pray; grant thou, lest faith turn to despair.

Much of the witty wordplay in Shakespeare is wanton and somewhat aggressive. The liveliest exchanges are between lovers who fight their way to the altar, where the wordplay is usually both seductive and initially hostile. The best example of this is in *Much Ado About Nothing*, where Benedick and Beatrice indulge in verbal sorties. Each is attracted to the other, but each refuses to bend to convention, Beatrice refusing to play the submissive woman, and Benedick playing with the pun on horns, rejecting all women for fear of cuckoldom. But Beatrice gives much away when she criticizes Benedick for his dancing, claiming that he would "board" her. The first meaning here is that he would stamp on her feet, but the secondary meaning rings through.

There are times when Shakespeare's use of puns is so complex that a character has to ask for an explanation. For example, in *Twelfth Night* Maria warns Feste the clown that he will be punished by his lady Olivia for his failure to attend her at court: "My lady will have thee for thy absence." To which Feste retorts, "Let her have me, he that is well hanged in this world needs to fear no colours." The puns on "have me" and "well hanged" need no explanation, but Maria has to ask for an explanation of what Feste means by "colours." Feste responds that it means, in a battle, he fears no one, and Maria finally catches on that he is referring to the regimental flags used during battle, with perhaps a further pun on the "collars" of the hangman.

As should be apparent, Shakespeare's puns can be quite lewd. Some of the bawdiness occurs in seemingly innocuous phrases like "too much of a good thing," spoken by Rosalind to Orlando in *As You Like It*. In Shakespeare's day, "thing" was a common euphemism for genitalia.

Some scholars see sexual allusions everywhere in Shakespeare's work. Frankie Rubinstein in *Dictionary of Shakespeare's Sexual Puns and their Significance* claims that the following words all have sexual connotations: "abhor," "abominable," "about," "absolute," "abuse," "access," "accommodate," "acorn," "acquaint," "adventure," "advocate" and "affection," and we're not even halfway through the letter *A*! Arriving at the letter *S*, Rubinstein tells us that in Elizabethan vernacular the word "surgeon" refers to the treatment of venereal disease, and thus in *Julius Caesar*, when the cobbler states he is "a surgeon to old shoes," it was not shoes that were being mended, but the bottoms of whores.

Many of the sexual puns centre on women and their supposed licentiousness. In *Cymbeline* we have the situation where Jachimo has told Posthumous that his wife Imogen has been unfaithful. Jachimo manages to secrete himself in a trunk in Imogen's bedchamber and comes out at night to spy on the sleeping Imogen. He steals a bracelet that Posthumous has given to her as proof of her infidelity. He says that this "will force him think I have picked the lock, and taken the treasure of her honour." Here "pick the lock" of course refers to the act of deflowering.

A similar sort of play on words occurs in *Hamlet* when the Prince refers to Polonius as a "fishmonger." He is angry because he believes Polonius is using Ophelia to gain information about his supposed madness. (In many productions, Hamlet is shown seeing Polonious hiding behind a curtain as Ophelia questions him.) The term "fish" was used in the sixteenth century as an off-colour allusion to a woman. Hence, Hamlet is essentially calling Polonius a pimp, a seller (monger) of women in that he is using his daughter to question Hamlet.

Many of Shakespeare's puns would nowadays be considered groaners. On the other hand, the fact that so many people enjoy bad puns shows that they serve a purpose and even contribute to a sense of community, for they transcend class distinctions. One should remember that Shakespeare is also employing them as a device to release tension in an audience, as is the case of the Porter in *Macbeth* after the murder of Duncan.

Puns also serve an important psychological function as a denial of anxiety. Shakespearean characters use puns in this manner, none more so than Hamlet. In *Shakespeare's Wordplay*, Molly Mahood writes that at times "Hamlet's wordplay does double duty by both masking his hostility towards Claudius and affording him a safety-valve for his bitterness at his mother's guilt." Prince Hamlet is forced to quibble and speak in ambiguous language lest he utter something overtly treasonous. The first encounter of Hamlet and Claudius highlights Hamlet's clever use of words. Claudius tries to placate Hamlet by addressing him as "my Cosin Hamlet, and my sonne." Hamlet then quips, "A little more than kin, and lesse than kind." Here, "kind" possesses at least three meanings. It could be implying that Claudius is less than a direct blood relation, "kind" meaning "ancestral stock." "Kind" also meant "natural," and Hamlet could be alluding to Claudius's unnatural lust. And, of course, "kind" in Shakespeare's era also had the modern sense of "considerate."

In addition, since *Hamlet* is in many ways an elaborate detective story, Shakespeare has developed many of the utterances by other characters as deliberately ambiguous, making it difficult for an audience to detect their intent. Hence, in the ghost scene Horatio says that he fears that the apparition "bodes some strange eruptions to our state." The "eruptions" can refer to a possible invasion of the "state" of Denmark by Norway, or to how regicide has disrupted the natural "state" of life.

Puns are also a theatrical device, with the interplay of words representing a linguistic duel for an audience to savour. In *Shakespearean Meanings*, Sigurd Burckhardt writes that a pun was used by Shakespeare to deny "the meaningfulness of words and so calls into question the genuineness of the linguistic currency on which the social order depends." Molly Mahood, in *Shakespeare's Wordplay*, proffers the belief that the Bard played with "verbal meanings, not because the rhetoricians approve of wordplay, but because his imagination as a poet works through puns, or his characters are placed in situations where it is natural for them to pun, or because puns help to clarify the particular view of life that he seeks to present in a particular play."

Sister Miriam Joseph in *Shakespeare's Use of the Arts of Language* indicates that Shakespeare's puns involve four forms of Renaissance rhetoric: antanaclasis, syllepsis, paronomasia and asteismus. Joseph explains that these rhetorical devices involve the logical distinction between the various meanings of a word. Their effect, she contends, depends on an intellectual alertness that allows one to perceive the ambiguity.

According to Sister Joseph, antanaclasis involves a figure of speech in which the same word is repeated in a different, if not contrary signification. In *Othello*, we see this passage: "Put out the light, then put out the light." On one hand, the "light" merely refers to the extinguishing of candles; its other sense refers to the murder of Desdemona.

In syllepsis, a word, or a particular form or inflexion of a word, is made to refer to two or more other words in the same sentence. An example of this occurs in *Hamlet* when Queen Gertrude tells Hamlet that death is "common." When Hamlet responds, "Ay, madam, it is common," he is making a cryptic reference that he regards his mother's marriage to Claudius so soon after the death of her husband to be highly improper.

Paranomasia is essentially a term for a pun as it refers to wordplay based on words that sound alike. For example, in *Richard III*, the line "Now is the winter of our discontent / Made glorious summer by this Son of York," we have the interplay on the homonyms "son" and "sun."

Finally, we have asteismus, which can be genteel irony, or polite and ingenious mockery. We see this process in the following dialogue in *As You Like It*:

> JAQUES: "By my truth, I was seeking for a fool when I found you."
>
> ORLANDO: "He is drowned in the brook. Look but in and you shall see him."
>
> JAQUES: "There I shall see my own figure."
>
> ORLANDO: "Which I take to be either a fool or a cipher."

Jaques, the court wit, has here come up against Orlando, who has been deprived of his education by his jealous brother, but it is Orlando who comes off best, forcing Jaques to see his own "figure" in the pool as either a fool or a "cipher," in other words, a "zero."

It is intriguing to note that in twenty-three of Shakespeare's thirty-seven plays, more than half of the puns occur in the first two acts. This is because one role of wordplay is to present the conflicting issues for the audience through the different meanings of words. Once these are clear in the minds of the audience, the pun is no longer needed as much.

Often Shakespeare was not satisfied with making merely a single pun on a word. For example, in *Romeo and Juliet*, Romeo describes his beloved as "Beauty too rich for use, for earth too dear!" Here, "use" can mean "employment," "interest" and "wear and tear"; "earth" has the senses of "mortal life" and "the grave"; and "dear" means both "cherished" and "costly." Even the word "beauty" can, in the context of the play, be a pun on "booty." Shakespeare displays multiple puns again in the opening scene of *Timon of Athens*, where the Poet's story about Fortune is a prelude to the whole drama. Throughout the play, "fortune" can mean "wealth," "good or bad luck," or it can refer to the capricious goddess who causes lives to be ruined. Those who have amassed large fortunes are rarely fortunate. Timon tells his friends "Pray sit, more welcome are ye to my Fortunes, than my Fortunes to me."

❧ PUNS BY OTHER LITERARY GREATS

Lewis Carroll was another inveterate punster. In *Through the Looking Glass* we have this passage:

> Here the Red Queen began again. "Can you answer useful
> questions?" she said. "How is bread made?"
>
> "I know that!" Alice cried eagerly. "You take some flour —"
>
> "Where do you pick the flower?" the White Queen asked.
> "In a garden or in the hedges?"
>
> "Well, it isn't picked at all," Alice explained: "it's ground —"
>
> "How many acres of ground?" said the White Queen.
> "You mustn't leave out so many things. Fan her head!"
>
> The Red Queen anxiously interrupted. "She'll be feverish
> after so much thinking."

The puns that Carroll uses here are based on homophones and word ambiguities that are likely to be understood by a sharp ten-year-old. Other examples are when Alice tells the Duchess, "The earth takes twenty-four days to turn around on its axis." The Duchess retorts: "talking of axes — off with her head." And when the Mouse tells Alice, "Mine is a long and sad tale," Alice is confused and asks him why having a long tail makes him sad.

Centuries before Carroll, John Donne's three-verse poem "A Hymn to God the Father" displays some of his exquisite puns. The middle verse reads:

> Wilt thou forgive that sin which I have won
> Others to sin, and made my sin their door?
> Wilt Thou forgive that sin which I did shun
> A year or two, but wallowed in a score?
> When thou hast done, thou hast not done.
> For I have more.

The pun here is on Donne's own name, because the line "When thou hast done" can be heard as "When Thou hast Donne." There is another pun in the last verse where we read:

> I have a sin of fear, that when I have spun
> My last thread, I shall perish on the shore.

> But swear by Thyself, that at my death thy Son
> Shall shine as he shines now, and heretofore . . .

In other words, Donne is imploring God to provide him with the light of Christ, "his Son," who is also his "shining sun."

Oscar Wilde's *The Importance of Being Earnest* is another splendid literary source for puns, many of them serving the purpose of highlighting the narrow-mindedness and hypocrisy of Victorian society. In order to escape social expectations, the play's protagonist Jack Worthing creates a black sheep of a brother named Ernest, whose identity he adopts to cover his libertine behaviour. Ironically, he desperately wants to marry the daughter of Lady Bracknell, Gwendolen, whose main interest in him is the name she knows him by — Ernest. Following farcical twists and turns, Jack learns he was in fact christened Ernest. This discovery secures Gwendolen's affection and leads Jack to close the play in a pun by saying, "I've now realised for the first time in my life the vital Importance of Being Earnest."

For pure comic content, however, my favourite pun in the play is this famous quip by Lady Bracknell: "To lose one parent, Mr. Worthing, is a misfortune; to lose both looks like carelessness." This pun plays on the dual senses of "lose" as "misplace" and "have a loved one die."

As has been seen, however, not all punning in English literature is appreciated. Some commentators have found the plethora of puns in James Joyce's two masterpieces *Ulysses* and *Finnegans Wake* to be off-putting, but Joyce was unapologetic on this matter. He countered, "After all, the Holy Roman Catholic Apostolic Church was built on a pun," referring to the aforementioned quip by Jesus in Matthew 16:18: "Thou art Peter (Greek *Petros*), and upon this rock (Greek *petra*) I will build my Church." When asked whether many of the puns in *Ulysses* and *Finnegans Wake* were in essence trivial, he joyously retorted with a pun: "Yes some of them are trivial and some of them are quadrivial." In other words, they have at least four sources, not three ("trivial" literally means "three roads").

Not surprisingly, many of Joyce's puns were rather naughty and at times he even "out-bawdied" Shakespeare. For example, in *Ulysses* we find this little poem:

If you see kay
Tell him he may
See you in tea
Tell him for me.

The words of this ditty (particularly the first and third lines) when spoken phonetically (for example, in the third line, See = C) spell out two rather crude four-letter words that are apparent to the trenchant reader.

As further testimony to Joyce's love of puns, in one scene of *Ulysses*, his protagonist Leopold Bloom recalls this complex statement by English logician Richard Whately that includes four puns: "Why can a man never starve in the Great Desert? Because he can eat the sand which is there. But what brought the sandwiches there? Why, Noah sent Ham and his descendants mustered and bred." The four puns here are "sand which" / "sandwich," "Ham" / "ham," "mustered" / "mustard" and "bred" / "bread." Joyce obviously relished mustard puns, for in *Finnegans Wake* we see this line, "Lard have mustard on them." (See Part I, Chapter 6 for an analysis of Joyce's puns on his characters' names.)

Whether curmudgeons like it or not, many jokes rely on language play, and the vast majority of these include punnery in some form. But aside from the reality and large presence of puns, a pun often symbolizes a universe of possibility. It reshapes the language we use to describe the world, and in that sense can be seen as a political gesture, even a revolutionary one. Shared laughter aimed at a common enemy can be a catalyst to boldness.

HAVE PUNS NOT GUNS: POLITICAL PUNSTERS

French linguist Pierre Guiraud stated, "Puns are one of the main weapons of political satire under dictatorships. They flourish during wars of religion, the Revolution, the Occupation and, nearer our time, in most police states." American essayist Peter De Vries, in *Without a Stitch in Time*, stated that puns "arise from one of the most intense forms of belligerence — the belligerence of the insecure." In his book *Jokes*, British essayist C.P. Wilson is referring specifically to jokes but his idea applies also to puns: "Joking reflects and . . . compensates for our failings . . . and self-alienation. Freed from ignorance, inhibitions, fear and prejudice, the super-psyche would have no use for humour."

A pun during Leonid Brezhnev's Soviet regime declared that there was no news in *Pravda* ("truth" in Russian) and no truth in *Izvestia* ("news" in Russian). Similarly, the underground in Nazi Germany featured *Flusterwize*, "whispered jokes." One of the best ones presented a German looking at portraits of Göbbels, Göring and Hitler, and musing: "Should one hang them or put them against the wall." This "hanging" motif was also used by Benjamin Franklin upon signing the Declaration of Independence when he quipped, "We must all hang together, or assuredly we shall all hang separately."

What is art in the Bard's deft hand or that of other literary lions can be downright maddening when abused by lesser mortals. Oliver Wendell Holmes suggested that killing a punster was warranted if the pun is bad enough. This view is reminiscent of the story told of a king who decides not to hang his jester if only the fool will foreswear puns. The jester responds "no noose is good news," so the king hangs him.

❧ PUNGENT PUNS BY LADIES & GENTS

In addition to literary and political punsters, there are well-known and not so well-known wags who have bequeathed the language both sublime and ridiculous puns:

Groucho Marx — Time wounds all heels.

Chico Marx — When someone exclaimed "Eureka," he shot back, "You donna smella so good yourself."

Edgar Bergen — Show me where Stalin's buried and I'll show you a Communist plot.

Max Eastman — One of the advantages of nuclear war is that all men are cremated equal.

Dorothy Parker (asked to give a sentence with the word horticulture) — You can lead a horticulture but you can't make her think.

The things my wife buys at auctions are
keeping me baroque.

H.L. Mencken — Television is like a steak: a medium rarely
well done.

Oliver Wendell Holmes Sr. — As a physician, I am grateful
for small fevers.

Peter De Vries — The things my wife buys at auctions are
keeping me baroque.

Zsa Zsa Gabor — I am a very good housekeeper. Every time
I get divorced, I keep the house.

George Carlin — Atheism is a non-profit organization.

Sir Walter Scott — Please return my book. I find that
though many of my friends are poor arithmeticians, they are
nearly all good bookkeepers.

Ronald Reagan — During arms talks with Mikhail
Gorbachev, the American president quipped, "It was
a proposal, one might say, disarmingly simple."

Marie Lloyd — The songwriter and music-hall singer heard
several complaints about her song title "She Sits Among the
Cabbages and Peas." Being an obliging sort, she changed the
title to "She Sits Among the Cabbages and Leeks."

It's probably clear by now that the basis of virtually all puns, and many
jokes, is the homonym, which lulls us into thinking about a word in a
certain context only to surprise us at the punch line where a second un-
expected meaning comes into play. When I was six years old, the first
riddle I was told by my Uncle Bernard featured a homonym:

"What has four wheels and flies?"
Answer: A garbage truck.

When I entered pre-pubescence, it was deemed proper by this same
pun-loving uncle to pose the following more risqué riddle to me:

"Why do firemen have bigger balls than policeman?"
Answer: Because they sell more tickets.

So, thanks in large part to my Uncle Bernard, I acquired a love of puns
at an early age and have noticed that, as with jokes in general, certain
categories have become particularly popular for punning.

ℵ COMMERCIAL PUNS

Puns are often featured as an advertising tool for a simple reason. Money.
Advertising space is costly and puns are economical because one receives
two pearls of wisdom for the price of one. Here are some clever ones I've
spotted or that have been brought to my attention:

Baby supplies — Rock a dry baby.

Beauty salon — Enter the best little hair house in town.

Butcher shop — We will sell no swine before its time.
(In the 1970s, "We will sell no wine before its time" was
the slogan of Paul Masson Wine.)

Electrician — Let us remove your shorts.

Hardware store — Picks up where your dog leaves off
(promoting a pooper-scooper).

Music shop — Gone Chopin. Bach in a minuet.

Plumber — A flush is better than a full house & You
don't have to sleep with a drip tonight.

Sporting goods store — Now is the winter of our
discount tents.

Steel fabrication company — Our erections never fail.

ଞ CORPORATE PUNS

Because they are so memorable, puns are often used as slogans for busi-
nesses:

Durex Condoms — More bang for your buck.

The Economist — For top laps.

Hebrew National Hot Dog — No ands, ifs, or butts.

IBM — I think, therefore IBM.

John Deere Tractors — Nothing runs like a Deere.

One-Second Plumber — Helps the drains run on time.

Springmaid Sheets — A buck well spent on a Springmaid
Sheet. (This ad featured an Amerindian lass stepping out of
a hammock made of a sheet, while an Amerindian lad is
lying on the hammock in a state of total exhaustion.)

Taco Bell — Think outside the bun.

Tic Tac Candy — Tic Tac. Surely the best tactic.

Weight Watchers — Taste. Not waist.

Wendy's — Where's the beef?

And if the manufacturers of any of the pills for erectile dysfunction are ever able to convert their product to a liquid form, I have the perfect slogan for them: *Pour yourself a stiff one.*

✕ BILINGUAL PUNS

Knowledge of other languages allows for bilingual puns, such as the ones below. (Given my Quebec origins, they are mostly from French.)

Did you hear about the snail automobile race? When the snail with the letter *S* painted on his car pulled ahead, spectators exclaimed, "Look at that *S car go*!" (play on *snail* in French — *escargot*)

Did you hear about the French chef who committed suicide? He lost the *huile d'olive*. (play on *will to live*)

French food never has two eggs in it, because one egg is always *un oeuf*. (play on *enough*)

Although some French pedants look down on the pun because of its inherent lack of clarity, puns are an important source of French jokes, such as this one ostensibly stated by Napoleon: *"Ma sacré toux!"* (My goddamn cough!) An underling thinks his commander has said *"Massacrez tout!"* (Massacre everything) and hence murders all the villagers.

A supposed incomplete knowledge of French can lead a wordsmith to define some French expressions incorrectly:

Carte Blanche — Blanche is too drunk to walk

Mets Chinois — Chinese baseball team

Suivre la *piste* — Follow the intoxicated woman

From my Jewish background comes the Hebrew word *sefer* meaning "book" and the term *sefer torah* referring to the Torah scrolls. This leads to the pun:

> What do you get when you cross a condom with a Torah?
> Answer: A *safer* Torah.

⅋ PRONUNCIATION PUN

The pronunciation of words, especially the names of people, often leads to some hilarious situations:

> It may not be so well-known, but Ronald Reagan changed the pronunciation of his surname from *Reegun* to *Raygun*. This transformation led to Lyndon Baines Johnson's quip, "If Ronald Reagan can call himself *Raygun*, I'm gonna call my beagles, *bagels*."

⅋ GRAMMATICAL PUNS

Grammar and sexuality do not seem obvious companions, but on occasion they work with unusual results:

> A woman picks up a cab at Boston Airport and asks, "Can you tell me where I can get scrod [whitefish]." The cabby replies, "Hey, I've never heard it expressed before in the pluperfect subjunctive."

> The mistress of a gangster completes her stint at a finishing school. She is picked up by her boyfriend who asks, "Were you blue when I was away?" The mobster slaps her on the face and says, "A year in finishing school and you didn't learn it should be 'blown'?"

⅋ PUNCTUATION PUNS

Of all the puns of recent date, the following pun on punctuation may well have had the widest circulation — certainly among book lovers:

A panda walks into a café, orders a sandwich, eats it, then whips out a pistol and shoots the waiter in the leg. "Why?" implores the grazed server. The panda shrugs, tosses him a badly punctuated wildlife manual and walks out. When the bleeding waiter skims the book he finds out the reason he was assaulted. "Panda: Large, black and white; native to China. Eats, shoots and leaves." (This pun was made famous as the title of Lynne Truss's 2003 best-seller *Eats Shoots & Leaves*.)

✸ ANIMAL PUNS

From time immemorial lovers of language have enjoyed playing with the lore surrounding animals:

How do you get down from an elephant? You don't, you get *down* from a duck.

One early morning, a farmer was milking his cow. The farmer was just starting to get a good rhythm going when a fly flew into the barn and started circling his head. Suddenly, the bug flew into the cow's ear. The farmer didn't think much about it, until the bug squirted out into his bucket. It went in one ear and out the *udder*!

✸ BAR PUNS

One of the most popular forms of jokes and puns involves the bar scene, with all the possibilities there for slightly tipsy reasoning, although often the results can be groaners:

A three-legged dog walks into a saloon in the Old West. He sidles up to the bar and announces: "I'm looking for the man who shot my *paw*."

A string walks into a bar and orders a drink. Looking at the string, the bartender says, "Sorry, we don't serve strings here." The string decides not to take offence at

this egregious example of fabric profiling, and proceeds
to the bathroom, rearranges his end, comes back out and
approaches the bar again to order a drink. "Hey, ain't
you that friggin' string?" asks the bartender. "Nope.
I'm a frayed knot."

I'm looking for the man who shot my paw.

℣ CRIME PUNS

The underworld of criminals certainly has given rise to numerous puns,
many of which depend on the lack of intellectual wherewithal of either
the criminal or the police:

A thief breaks into the local police station and steals all the
toilets and urinals, leaving no clues. A CSI spokesperson was
quoted as saying, "We have absolutely nothing to *go on*."

An aspiring hit man named Artie wants to earn himself a reputation, so he decides to make his first contract hit for only one dollar. He follows his target into a supermarket and, when he believes he is alone with him, he strangles the man. Much to his chagrin, he notices an elderly couple had witnessed the act. He deems it necessary to strangle both of them to eliminate any witnesses. Of course the security cameras nail him and he is subsequently arrested. The next day's headline read: "ARTIE CHOKES 3 FOR A DOLLAR AT A&P."

Recently a thief in Paris almost got away with stealing several paintings from the Louvre. However, after planning the crime, getting in and out past security, he was captured only two blocks away when his SUV ran out of gas. When asked how he could mastermind such a brilliant crime and then make such an idiotic mistake, he replied: "I had no *Monet* to buy *Degas* to make the *Van Gogh*."

✵ HEALTH CARE PUNS

The doctor's office is frequently a splendid place to find puns. The staff appear to delight in posting medical put-downs.

A man walks into a psychiatrist's office wearing only underwear made of Saran Wrap. The psychiatrist says, "Well, I can clearly see *your* nuts."

A man rushed into the doctor's office and shouted, "Doctor! I think I'm shrinking!" The doctor calmly responded, "Now, settle down. You'll just have to be a *little patient*."

Did you hear about the Buddhist who refused Novocain during a root canal? His goal: to *transcend dental medication*.

✵ MUSIC PUN

Composers have a great love of musical jokes. The scherzo, the fast light movement in a symphony, embodies jocularity. Actual jokes in music are also not uncommon. Mozart's Ein Musikalischer Spaß (A Musical Joke K: 522) is among the most famous. This "Divertimento for Two Horns and String Quartet" has intentional harmonic and rhythmic mistakes which serve to parody the work of incompetent composers. The asymmetrical phrasing at the beginning of the first movement is a prime example which, when recognized, brings many smiles to the faces of the listening audience. The following is a more literary joke drawing on musical terminology:

> C, E-flat, and G go into a bar. The bartender says, "Sorry, but we don't serve minors." So E-flat leaves, and C and G have an open fifth between them. After a few drinks, the fifth is diminished, and G is out flat. F comes in and tries to augment the situation, but is not sharp enough. D comes in and heads for the bathroom, saying, "Excuse me; I'll just be a second." Then A comes in, but the bartender is not convinced that this relative of C is not a minor. Then the bartender notices B-flat hiding at the end of the bar and says, "Get out! You're the seventh minor I've found in this bar tonight." E-flat comes back the next night in a three-piece suit with nicely shined shoes. The bartender says, "You're looking sharp tonight. Come on in, this could be a major development." Sure enough, E-flat soon takes off his suit and everything else, and is *au natural*. Eventually C sobers up and realizes in horror that he's under a rest. C is brought to trial, found guilty of contributing to the diminution of a minor, and is sentenced to 10 years of D.S. without Coda at an upscale correctional facility.

℘ PUNS FROM FICTION

Puns from the literary world we have already seen in abundance from Shakespeare to James Joyce, but there are many others from lesser names, and I fear of lesser quality:

> Quasimodo, the cerebrally challenged bell ringer of Notre Dame, puts an ad in the newspaper for an assistant. One

man applies for the job but he has no arms. "How are you going to assist me?" asks Quasimodo. "No sweat" replies the man and he runs hard towards the bell and smashes it with his head. BONG! "Awesome!" says Quasimodo. "Could you show me that again?" "Sure!" says the man and he charges the bell again but misses the swinging bell and falls out of the bell tower. A crowd huddles around the hapless man lying in the street, and a police officer inquires, "Does anyone know who he is?" Quasimodo emerges and says, "I don't know his name, but his face sure *rings a bell*!"

The day after the armless man fell to his death, another chap shows up and states that he is the brother of the armless man and he wants to audition for the bell ringer's job. Quasimodo takes him to the bell tower whereupon the guy picks up the wooden mallet and starts to ring the bell. He takes a mighty swing, misses the bell and plummets over the balcony to his death. Quasimodo scampers outside and the policeman asks him for the name of the deceased. Quasimodo says, "I never got his name but he's a *dead ringer* for his brother."

Dr. Watson arrives at 221B Baker Street and is stunned to find his friend Sherlock Holmes out front dressed in a mackintosh while applying a pale yellow gloss to the front door. "Holmes, what is it?" cried the stupefied Watson. "*A lemon entry*, my dear Watson."

✷ QUASI-SEXUAL PUNS

The bedroom, or what passes for it today, is clearly a place where the introduction of a pun would endanger the ongoing passion. But puns *about* sex have always been a great favourite:

Two brooms were hanging in the closet and after a while they became familiar with each other and decided to wed. Being traditional brooms, one broom was the bride broom and the other the groom broom. The bride broom looked very beautiful in her white dress; the groom broom was handsome and debonair in his tuxedo. The wedding was exquisite. At the reception, the bride broom leaned over and whispered to the groom broom, "I think I am going to have a little whisk broom." "Impossible," said the groom broom. "We haven't even *swept* together."

An old man takes a shortcut through an alley and is accosted by a busty wench clad in a rather short skirt leaning on a lamppost. She asks him, "Hey buddy. Care for some super sex?" He replies, "I'll take the *soup*."

⅋ RELIGIOUS PUNS

Today, puns about religion must be dealt with carefully as events in Paris have shown, although the Christian and Jewish religions seem to have been fair game — at least in the last one hundred years:

It's OK to kiss a nun as long as you don't *get into the habit*.

Why is there an Old Testament and a New Testament? Because even God *keeps two sets of books*.

⅋ SCIENCE PUNS

The world of scientists in their laboratories is, in my experience, usually one of dedicated professionals working close to 24-7, but on occasion even those in particle physics have their moments of levity:

Two hydrogen atoms meet. One says, "I've lost my electron." The other says "Are you sure?" The first replies, "Yes, *I'm positive*."

⅋ HEADLINE PUNS

Unfortunately, many puns we find in headlines are not particularly clever and feel forced, and therefore should be avoided. Examples of such are the following:

Mumps outbreak *swells*

Bell's name doesn't have a familiar *ring* for many voters

Francis names a *flock of new cardinals*

On the other hand, sometimes we find gems. The following are samples:

In the 1934 World Series, pitcher Dizzy Dean, not known for his sterling intellect, tried to break up a double play and was hit on the head by the baseball in the process. He was rushed to hospital but wasn't seriously injured. The next day the headline in the *St. Louis Globe-Democrat* read, "X-rays of Dean's Head *Reveal Nothing*."

The headline "Britannia *Waives the Rules*" has appeared quite often in a variety of contexts when a headline writer wants to express indignation over some decision Great Britain has made. Not surprisingly, it has been used especially in Irish and Scottish newspapers. In a twist on this, one year, the USA schooner lost to the British in an America's Cup race, but the USA team effected a retroactive change in the rules thereby disqualifying the British. In response, a British newspaper ran this headline: "Britannia Rules the Waves But America *Waives the Rules*."

In Sydney, Australia, a newspaper story dealt with gourmet kangaroo meat. The headline read "A *Roo* Awakening at the Table."

When actress Renée Zellwegger, star of *Bridget Jones' Diary*, got married a headline read "Bridget Jones' *Dowry*."

One British daily ran a column on the resignation of a minister of the British government. The headline in *Marxism Today* read "On a *Whinge* and a Prayer."

When the Taliban was in power in Afghanistan, they decreed that no music could be played in public. This edict was defied by some brave souls prompting *The Guardian* to run the headline "The *Banned* Played On."

When Pole Czesław Miłosz won the Nobel Prize in
Literature in 1980 *Time* magazine's headline was
"Honoring a *Pole Apart*."

Sometimes the headlines depend on the reader knowing some cultural reference that must be understood before trying to understand a pun. For example, the expression "Dutch courage" refers to courage one receives after drinking alcohol. When the Euro was introduced into the Netherlands, a British daily ran this headline: "Dutch Take Courage and Prepare for the Euro." Similarly, the headline "Why the Clyde Offer is Not So Bonny," which dealt with a takeover offer from a Scottish company named Clyde, could leave readers perplexed if they didn't realize that it is a pun on the movie *Bonnie and Clyde*, as well as the word "bonny" that means "pleasant to the sight" in Scottish English. A sports headline was used for a story that dealt with the remote chances of the Welsh rugby team beating the South African team. It only works if one knows that the nickname of the South African team is the Springboks, or Boks, for short: "Between a *Bok* and a Hard Place."

Similarly, a headline that ran in the *Indianapolis Star* May 8, 1974, "Nixon to Stand Pat on Watergate Tapes," works only if one is aware that Richard Nixon's wife was named Pat. In February 2008, the then Archbishop of Canterbury, Rowan Williams, stated that some elements of Islamic Sharia law should be introduced in Britain. This stance elicited a photograph of Williams in the *Sun* the following day with this headline: "What a Burqa!" One has to know that *berk* is a British term for an idiot, but it is the origin of the term that made its use particularly offensive. The term *berk* derives from Cockney slang in which Berkshire *Hunt* substitutes for a part of the female anatomy.

Finally, one of my all-time favourite punning headlines was spotted some years ago when the Scottish soccer team Caley Thistle scored a major upset over powerhouse Celtic. The headline in the *Scottish Sun* read "Super Caley Go Ballistic, Celtic Are Atrocious."

In conclusion, what constitutes a great pun is largely subjective. Here are two of my current favourites:

A timid husband is unable to buy his wife's preferred
anemones for her birthday and fearfully returns home

bearing some greenery. To his surprise she gushes, "With fronds like these who needs anemones?"

A woman had twins and gave them up for adoption. One of them went to an Egyptian family who named him Amal. The other was adopted by a Spanish family who called him Juan. Years later, Juan sends a picture of himself to his birth mother. She tells her husband that she would also like to have a photograph of Amal. Her husband responds, "But they're twins! If you've seen Juan, you've seen Amal."

As Charles Lamb was mentioned earlier, I would like to give him the last word. The inveterate punster said that "a pun is a pistol let off at the ear; not a feather to tickle the intellect." I agree that many puns are in bad taste, but bad taste is our typical haunt for humour, and puns represent a distinct way of feeling and thinking that shouldn't be ignored. Puns also illuminate the nature of language. They are a resource of language, and certain temperaments can't resist mining and exploiting its rich ore. They are also a fixture of the flexibility of the English language and I believe should be celebrated by all English-speaking logophiles.

ଔ ଔ ଔ

It is now time for readers to participate in the pun-fest.

ଔ HOMONYM PUZZLE

As homonyms are the lifeblood of puns, readers are asked to decipher all these animal homonym phrases.

PHRASE	ANSWER
Example: Female insect relation	ant/aunt
1 Insect twitch	_____
2 Entomological power	_____
3 Merit a sea eagle	_____
4 Macho mollusk display	_____

5   Moby Dick's lament   _____

6   Kermit the frog lost his parking spot   _____

7   Spirit of fish   _____

8   Expensive doe   _____

9   Bambi's bread   _____

10 Bullwinkle in a blender   _____

11 Tabloid for antelopes   _____

12 Rabbit fur   _____

13 Fibbin' feline   _____

14 Golf course for wildcats   _____

15 Cat that uses steroids (in Brooklynese)   _____

16 Female horse's French mother   _____

17 Nay a neigh   _____

18 Long-winded pig   _____

19 Irregular simian warrior   _____

ANSWERS: p. 144

Tabloid for antelopes.

᪥ DOUBLE MEANING PUZZLE

Test your mettle on words with different meanings by trying to solve the
following clues. To help you, the answers appear in alphabetical order.

CLUE	ANSWER
Example: Even cravat	tie
1 Unreturned service card	_____
2 Spheroid dance	_____
3 Tolerate polar	_____
4 Outscore rhythm	_____
5 Beak charge	_____
6 Colours depression	_____
7 Cliff deception	_____
8 Dog teeth	_____
9 Red bird number	_____
10 Reason for which a person fights	_____
11 Eggs on toast	_____
12 Train or bus	_____
13 Succeed effortlessly at water's edge	_____
14 Mixed company	_____
15 Penny swiper	_____
16 Rural area nation	_____
17 Justice hall playing area	_____
18 Smack sleeve end	_____
19 Projectile dash	_____
20 Hyphen run	_____
21 See a fruit	_____
22 Illustrate extract	_____
23 Underwear designers	_____
24 Fascinate way in	_____
25 Rash outburst	_____
26 Take advantage of an adventure	_____
27 Even apartment	_____
28 Liberate without cost	_____

29 Level poker hand   _____

30 Sympathetic character   _____

ANSWERS: p. 144

⚔ CRYPTIC HOMONYM PUZZLE

One of the reasons English is a devilishly difficult language to master is because words can have so many different meanings. The best examples are the words "set" and "run." Both can be used as adjectives, nouns and verbs, and there are over 400 different senses to each word in the *OED*. On the positive side, words that have double meanings are a staple of cryptic crossword puzzles in which puns figure prominently. A typical clue is "season well" whose answer is "spring" because spring refers to both a "season" and a "well." To help you, the number of letters in the answer is given. See if you can solve the following cryptic clues to these puns.

CLUE	ANSWER
Example: Reduced to bankruptcy in dilapidated old building (4)	ruin
1 Operate a race (3)	_____
2 Desire for Japanese money (3)	_____
3 Ban pub (3)	_____
4 Diploma for measuring temperature (6)	_____
5 Boom box (4)	_____
6 Satisfaction of many lions (5)	_____
7 Catch on to a stick (4)	_____
8 Dresser agency (6)	_____
9 Depend on financial institution (4)	_____
10 Encourage baby bird (3)	_____
11 Hit the juice (5)	_____
12 Large excavation owned by me (4)	_____
13 Metal guide (4)	_____
14 Young ladies are not hits (6)	_____
15 Hold back stalk (4)	_____
16 Small and perfect (5)	_____

17 Cover for head gangster (4)   _____
18 Trim a tree (6)   _____
19 Signify base (4)   _____
20 Small child (5)   _____
21 Meaty complaint (4)   _____
22 Press club (4)   _____
23 Fish struggle awkwardly (8)   _____
24 Lemon chicken (6)   _____
25 Burning discharge (6)   _____
26 Banked left (9)   _____
27 Boot wax for Eastern Europe (6)   _____
28 Very small amount of time (6)   _____

ANSWERS: p. 145

It should be apparent that we delight in arranging language to appear clever and witty. You will discover that what can appear to be "deranged" language is often actually rather artfully orchestrated. The previous chapter's "pure" puns become transpositional ones as letters, syllables and even whole words shift place in the next chapter.

CHAPTER 2

ȣ

Spoonerisms

"It takes brains and creativity to patch a Hun."
— Robert Schleifer

ȣ TIPS OF THE SLUNG

Was that pun deliberate or accidental? Some wit lulls the hearer into believing that a genuine mistake has occurred whereas, in fact, the error has been artfully choreographed. Such is often the case with spoonerisms, which, like malaprops, are named after a person, but unlike the literary creation of Mrs. Malaprop there was a real flesh and blood Spooner. We get the word "spoonerism" from the Reverend William Archibald Spooner, who was Dean at New College in Oxford from 1876 to 1889, and Warden there between 1903 and 1924.

The first citation of "spoonerism" in the *OED* dates to 1900, but the *OED* mentions that the word had been in colloquial use at Oxford since 1885. Spooner was a highly respected administrator responsible for many reforms, but history has been unkind to the dear Reverend, for he is not remembered for his forward thinking but for his involuntary metatheses, or linguistic reversals. These have come to be called "spoonerisms," and with the good Dean they were always accidental slips and never contrived. In the nineteenth century some people used the term "marrowsky" for these transpositional puns. The term supposedly came from a mysterious Count Marrowsky who used similarly to mangle the English language in London during the eighteenth century. The term "marrowsky," however, has become archaic within the last century.

It has been reported that Spooner once referred to the title of the hymn "Conquering Kings Their Titles Take" as "Kinkering Congs," and introduced Dr. Childe's friend as "Dr. Friend's child." The reversals were not limited to words. At a dinner party he is said to have upset salt and then poured red wine on the salt. One might say that in both words and deeds he "put the heart before the course."

There is a dearth of documented gaffes by this unfortunate eponymous administrator, but this did not stop his supposed unintentional bloopers from becoming the stuff of legend to sophomoric Oxonians with "mad banners." During a wedding at which he officiated he supposedly blathered, "If anyone present knows why this couple shouldn't be *joyfully loined* together" and later "it is *kisstomary* to *cuss* the bride."

It is kisstomary to cuss the bride.

Defenders of Spooner maintain that some of the alleged howlers attributed to him are a *lack of pies*. They include the following:

I have in my bosom a *half-warmed fish* (half-formed wish).

A toast which needs no commendation from me: our *queer Dean* (dear Queen).

The Lord is a *shoving leopard* (loving shepherd).

I've just *hanged* (banged) my *bed* (head).

You are *occupewing the wrong pie* (occupying the wrong pew).

May I sew you to another sheet? (may I show you to another seat).

Ow! I hit my *bunny phone* (funny bone).

Is the *bean dizzy?* (Dean busy).

May *sod* (God) rest his *goal* (soul).

I *remember your name* perfectly, but I *can't think of your face*.

You have *hissed* (missed) all my *mystery* (history) lectures and *tasted* two *worms* (wasted two terms). I saw you *fight* (light) a *liar* (fire). Pack up your *rags* (bags) and *bugs* (rugs), and leave immediately by the *town drain* (down train).

I have never before addressed so many *tons of soil* (sons of toil — to a group of farmers).

As you can see from the above examples, the linguistic reversals we find in spoonerisms take different forms. The most common exchange involves the initial sounds of words (invariably consonants) which can be classified as phonemic transpositions: "tons of soil"/"sons of toil." Next there are syllabic transpositions: "occupewing the wrong pie"/"occupying the wrong pew." Lastly, there are lexical transpositions: "fat of the land"/ "land of the fat."

Although the word "spoonerism" only surfaces at the beginning of the twentieth century, the concept of the transpositional pun in English goes back to the seventeenth century, notwithstanding that a well-established word did not yet exist for it. In Henry Peacham's 1622 *Peacham's Compleat Gentleman* we find this passage: "A melancholy gentleman, sitting one day at a table where I was, started up upon the sudden and, meaning to say, '*I must go buy a dagger*,' by transposition of the letters, said: '*Sir, I must go dye a beggar*.'"

What causes the accidental linguistic gaffes, when they are indeed accidental? Sigmund Freud viewed these slips of the tongue as symptomatic of unconscious forces or mental conflict deep in the psyche. Freud's interpretation, however, doesn't account for the majority of gaffes, which are not particularly dramatic, such as saying "right lane" instead of "light rain." More plausible is the explanation provided by Laurence Goldstein, a philosophy professor at the University of Kent. He believes the errors are "due to interference of the preparatory processing of sounds soon to be produced. . . . We appear to think ahead to the sounds we shall need to make."

Over time, the spoonerism has permeated popular culture in a myriad of ways and has been adopted as a popular comedic device. The *Monty Python* comedy troupe made particularly memorable use of spoonerisms. Who can forget the skit in which a customer walks into a bookshop and asks the proprietor if he has a *Sale of Two Titties* by Darles Chickens?

The appeal in arranged spoonerisms lies in the mind's seeking symmetry and balance. In perceiving both sides of the equation, there is a sense of completion or resolution. For example, take the joke "What's the difference between a rooster and a lawyer?" Answer: "The rooster *clucks defiance*. . . ." The joke only works if the listener can make the correct linguistic transposal and share in the satisfaction of transposing that the lawyer f***s the clients. Perhaps, the only one not amused is the effing attorney. Similarly, to understand Oscar Wilde's quip, "Working is the curse of the drinking class," one must know to transpose the gerunds "working" and "drinking."

So we do find in English some clever bawdy spooneristic jokes, but by and large English must take a back seat to French in bawdy word transposals. *Contrepèterie*, as it is called in French, goes back to the twelfth century. *Contrepèts* need not be lewd, but the most memorable ones are lusty. Rabelais is considered to be the father of the coarse variety. Here are some examples of Rabelaisian *contrepèterie*:

Femme *folle* à *la Messe* / *molle* à *la fesse*.
(The woman is crazy in Church / she has a soft ass.)

Les laborieuses *populations du cap* / *copulations du Pape*.
(The laborious populations of the Cape / the painstaking copulations of the Pope.)

Les Anglaises aiment *le tennis en pension* / *le pénis en tension*.
(English girls like tennis in their boarding school / are fond of erect penises.)

ಇ SPOONERISTIC DEFINITIONS

Spoonerisms occasionally render interestingly ironic definitions, and after reading the following list you might "spooneristically" ask yourself if you've *bred any good rooks* lately:

Alimony — Bounty from the mutiny.

Botanical discovery — A new lice on leaf (attributed to Ed Horr).

Bra — Bust blocker.

Champagne — Sips that passion the night.

Hangover — The wrath of grapes.

Psychologist — A person who pulls habits out of rats.

Racetracks — Where windows clean people (attributed to *Mad* magazine).

Truckers — De bigger dey are, de farder dey haul.

℅ SPOONERISTIC TITLES

Spoonerisms have at times been used as titles:

Too True to Be Good — A play by George Bernard Shaw.

Every Little Crook and Nanny — A novel by Evan Hunter.

You'll See It When You Believe It — A self-help book by Wayne Dyer.

The Hand that Cradles the Rock — A collection of poetry by Rita Mae Brown.

Blume in Love — A 1973 movie directed by Paul Mazursky starring George Segal.

Rock of the Westies — An album by Elton John.

One even sees spoonerisms in lyrics. In the song "Walk On" by U2 we hear "You're packing a suitcase for a place none of us has been, a place that has to be *believed to be seen*." My favourite sung spoonerism, however, is the titled lyric by Randy Hanzlick: *"I'd rather have a bottle in front of me than have a frontal lobotomy."* This phrase has been attributed to singer Tom Waits and apparently was first used in an interview with him.

℅ SHAGGY DOG STORIES

Sometimes transposition puns are used as punch lines to elaborate stories, usually referred to as "shaggy dog" stories, or stories that go on, seemingly endlessly. The first shaggy dog stories seem to have been variations on a tall tale that was indeed about a shaggy-haired dog. Wordsmith Eric Partridge wrote in 1953 in *The "Shaggy Dog" Story: Its Origin, Development and Nature* that "the best explanation of the term is that it arose in a story very widely circulated only since 1942 or 1943, although it was apparently invented in the 1930s." By and large, I find this genre far too contrived to be considered witty. But as many people enjoy this genre, I have included two of them.

The first concerns the Round Table:

Sir Lancelot was riding back to Camelot on a stormy night when his horse stumbled and broke a leg. He noticed a peasant's house and while knocking loudly on the door, he shouted, "I must return to the Round Table. Give me a horse." The peasant answered, "Sire, we have no horse but only a Great Dane." Lancelot replied, "I have no choice. Saddle up your cur and I'll ride him home." The peasant retorted, *"Sire, I wouldn't send a knight out on a dog like this."*

The second takes us to Africa:

An African chief is so beloved by his people that they bestow on him a dazzling jewel-laden ceremonial chair. At the ceremony, the chief expresses his gratitude and announces that the treasure will be reserved for high occasions of state.

Sire, I wouldn't send a knight out on a dog like this.

Hence, the gift is stored for safekeeping in the royal ware-hut. That night, however, tragedy strikes. The hut catches fire and all the contents therein are destroyed. Moral: *People who live in grass houses shouldn't stow thrones.*

Let me end this chapter with two of my favourite spoonerisms. One is a famous Edwardian spooneristic toast: Here's *cham*pagne to real friends . . . and *real pain* to *sham friends*. The other is a spooneristic ditty I created myself: A woman may play hard to get, while a man must *get hard to play*.

In the next chapter we will see how, at times, distinguishing wit from "nitwittery" represents a fool's (and often an Irish fool's) errand when concepts, rather than words alone, are manipulated. What appears to be an illogical statement can transcend its contradiction and ring true.

CHAPTER 3

⅋

Irish Bulls

"I can resist everything except temptation."
— Oscar Wilde

"I am not afraid of death; I just don't
want to be there when it happens."
— Woody Allen

⅋ GOOD OR BAD? CHAOTIC ORDER OR ORDERLY CHAOS?

After the previous chapters on puns and spoonerisms, most readers will probably have gleaned that one can't always distinguish a wit from a twit. Statements that are sometimes referred to as "Irish bulls," exemplify this classification problem.

An Irish bull refers to a pregnant statement that defies logic or syntax in some manner yet still manages to be communicative. You could say that an Irish bull delivers a vast idea in a half-vast manner. Here are two examples: "It was hereditary in his family to have no children," and the story of the Irish jury who returned with the verdict, "We find the man who stole the mare not guilty."

The origin of this sense of "bull" is obscure. Some have conjectured that it is connected to "papal bull" or with the Icelandic *bull*, "nonsense," but both these theories seem unlikely. My best guess is that the word is connected with either the Irish *buile*, "madness," or the Old French *boler/bouller*, "to deceive." Being common in Ireland, this form of wordplay is known as an "Irish" bull.

Alternate names for this phenomenon are "Goldwynism" and "Berraism" because of the penchant of movie mogul Samuel Goldwyn and former baseball player Yogi Berra for this type of statement.

Goldwyn (allegedly) made all of the following statements:

A verbal contract isn't worth the paper it's written on.

If I could drop dead right now, I'd be the happiest man alive.

A hospital is no place to be sick.

I can give you a definite perhaps.

We're overpaying him but he's worth it.

Don't talk to me while I'm interrupting.

The scene is dull. Tell him to put more life into his dying.

It isn't an optical illusion. It just looks like one.

Gentlemen, include me out!

A bachelor's life is no life for a single man.

Anyone who would go to a psychoanalyst should have his head examined!

Berra learned his métier under New York Yankees manager Casey Stengel, whose observations included comments, such as "A lot of people my age are dead at the present time," and "Good hitting always stops good pitching and vice versa." Berra is credited with the following:

Referring to a New York nightclub: nobody goes there anymore; it's too crowded.

Always go to other people's funerals; otherwise they won't come to yours.

90 percent of the game is half mental.

It's like déjà vu all over again.

It ain't over 'til it's over.

Many people think that Berra would have never employed the term *déjà vu*, it not being part of his vernacular. But Yogi swears he indeed used the French term in reference to regular home-runs hitters Roger Maris and Mickey Mantle.

MISCELLANEOUS IRISH BULLS

Here are some other utterances where the reader must decide if the content constitutes sense or nonsense:

Of course I can keep secrets. It's the people I tell them to that can't keep them. — Anthony Haden-Guest

The best cure for insomnia is to get a lot of sleep.
— W.C. Fields

We must believe in free will. We have no choice.
— Isaac Bashevis Singer

I must follow the people. Am I not their leader?
— Benjamin Disraeli

Hegel was right when he said that we learn from history that man can never learn anything from history.
— George Bernard Shaw

I always avoid prophesying beforehand because it is much better to prophesy after the event has already taken place.
— Winston Churchill

I am a deeply superficial person. — Andy Warhol

I wouldn't want to belong to any club that would have me as a member. — Groucho Marx

Thank God I'm an atheist. — Anonymous

Always be sincere, even when you don't mean it. — Irene Peter

Always be sincere, even when you don't mean it! —
"Darling, it's sooo slenderizing."

Despite the humour in such Irish bull types of statement, the *Gospel According to John* starts by acknowledging "In the Beginning was the Word." Hence, we have Biblical assurance that everything depends on single words, and in the next chapter we will examine the wordplay hidden in the supposed root of all knowledge — the word.

CHAPTER 4

৪

Word Definitions

"Wordplay hides a key to reality that the dictionary tries
in vain to lock inside every free word."
— Julio Cortázar, *Around the Day in Eighty Worlds*

৪ NEW MEANINGS FROM OLD WORDS

Standard puns usually rely on making comparisons based on homonyms
or with replaced rhymed words. A word re-defining punster uses a different modus operandi. Here, the meaning is interpreted based on the
sound of a word or by seeing the word divided in a distinct manner. Also,
he/she may create a word to describe some phenomenon for which there
is no word in existence.

In some cases we know the wag who re-defines a word, as in the following:

> Ambrose Bierce — one who drafts a plan of your house and
> plans a draft of your money (Architect)

Playboy magazine — a man who never has a bride idea (Bachelor)

Milton Berle — a group of men who spend hours taking minutes (Committee)

Oliver Herford — lying in state (Diplomacy)

John Wayne — Phony Express (Flattery)

Henry Morgan — one who can't help himself helping himself (Kleptomaniac)

William Safire — it's not the teat, it's the tumidity (Pornography)

However, as is the case with the following, often the wordplay is in common usage and the re-definer remains un-attributable:

Archaeologist — a man whose career lies in ruins

Egotist — one me-deep in conversation

Gossip — a person with a keen sense of rumour

Income Tax — capital punishment

Marriage — spouse trap

Middle age — when actions creak louder than words

Plea bargaining — using a proposition to end a sentence with

Shotgun wedding — a case of wife or death

On a lighter note, here is an alphabetical sampling of less profound lexical re-interpretations that are sometimes referred to as "daffy definitions":

Antimony — inheritance from your aunt

Brahman — female impersonator

Circumvent — opening in the front of boxer shorts
worn by Jewish men

Defibrillator — lie detector

Euthanasia — children of the Orient

Fungicide — killjoy

Gladiator — how the cannibal felt after having
the missionary lady for supper

Hijack — a tool for changing plane tires

Impotence — nature's way of saying "no hard feelings"

Jasmine — an underground tunnel where people
like cool music

Khakis — car keys in Boston

Liposuction — letting the fat out of the bag

Mistress — found between a mister and a mattress

Nitrate — cost of off-peak electricity

Oyster — Jewish complainer

Pesticide — killing of telemarketers

Rectitude — formal bearing adopted by a proctologist

Suicide — movement from depressed to deep rest

Toboggan — where you go for good deals

Urchin — lower part of a female's face

Vitamin — what you do when guests visit

Willy-nilly — impotent

Zebra — what a woman might wear after a silicon injection

৺ SPLIT DEFINITIVES

Some years ago I wrote two articles for the magazine *National Lampoon* that featured what I called "Split Definitives." These were words defined by dividing them into constituent parts and defining them by these parts. I then created a longer list of these word definitions for the language journal *Word Ways*. In some instances I collaborated with illustrators and had many of these hilarious illustrations published in a series of Canadian magazines. Divided into distinct categories, and presented alphabetically, here are some of these "split definitives":

৺ ANIMAL SPLIT DEFINITIVES

Archives — where Noah kept the bees

Bulldozer — somnolent viewer of a political debate

Catholic — compulsive cat lover

Damnation — beaver country

Ganglion — pack animal

Heathen — barbecued chicken

Insect — fashionable religious denomination

Medallion — top cat

Stagnation — deer country

Vamoose — elk in Virginia

Woodpecker — artificial penis

৺ GEOGRAPHIC, ETHNIC & HISTORICAL SPLIT DEFINITIVES

Audiology — science of German motoring

Calamity — L.A. relationship

Genitalia — highest Italian military rank

Hebrew — ballsy beer

Incandescent — what the Conquistadors cause

Lavatory — erupting Conservative

Maimonides — mugging of Caesar on March 15th

Netherlands — underworld

Polemist — fog over Warsaw

Redactor — target during the McCarthy hearings

Semitic — partial twitch

Tendons — conclave of Mafia bosses

Yosemite — funky greeting to a Jew or an Arab

❧ MISCELLANEOUS SPLIT DEFINITIVES

Addiction — Madison Avenues

Buccaneer — $2 earrings

Castrating — what a theatre critic does

Dozen — meditate

Execrating — Fortune 500

Fundamentalist — bankroll a psychic

Hearse — male buttocks

Inferno — imply a negative answer

Litany — question to an arsonist

Microwave — half-hearted farewell

Novices — spiritual perfection

Onus — we'll pay

Penalties — prison neckwear

Redolent — fast twice

Secretaries — hidden zodiac sign

Trifling — ménage à trois

Universe — poetic equivalent to a one-act play

Vicarious — priestly vow

Warrant — battle cry

Zither — female pimple

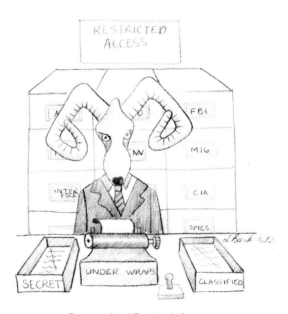

Secretaries / Secret Aries.

ℰ SPLIT DEFINITIVE ANIMAL PUZZLE

Now it's your turn. See how many of these split definitive clues you can decipher. They all feature words with hidden animals in them. To help you, the first letter and the number of letters in the word are provided.

CLUE	ANSWER
Example: Great hooter (S-9)	superbowl
	(superb&owl)

1	Run away and get married with a bug (A-8)	_____
2	Donkey was sick (A-8)	_____
3	Competent ursine creature (B-8)	_____
4	Nourished by a stinger (B-6)	_____
5	Somnolent viewer of an infomercial (B-10)	_____
6	Fire monkey (C-6)	_____
7	Compulsive cat lover (C-8)	_____
8	Dupe a mutt (C-6)	_____
9	Directed by a dairy animal (C-6)	_____
10	Watering hole for birds (C-7)	_____
11	Mangy dog's extremity (C-7)	_____
12	Protect bug (D-9)	_____
13	Large flightless bird that passed away (E-7)	_____
14	Anthropomorphic duck (M-8)	_____
15	Headquarters for burrowing mammal (M-11)	_____
16	Cat with eight legs (O-7)	_____
17	Shallow crossing for bovine draft animal (O-6)	_____
18	Vast amount of time for a swine (P-6)	_____
19	Paw (P-9)	_____
20	Cheap jewellery for a male sheep (R-8)	_____
21	Female rodent (R-6)	_____
22	Rodent atom (R-6)	_____
23	Big cat fighting for Dixie (R-9)	_____
24	Rabbit that works for a NY newspaper (T-9)	_____
25	Virginia elk (V-7)	_____

ANSWERS: p. 145

Although, as the Bible states, the word may be the beginning (sometimes of witty humour), the word can also create amusing wordplay in combinations. In the next chapter we will examine the phenomenon of how seemingly contradictory words can produce sublime truths when juxtaposed.

CHAPTER 5

§

Oxymoron

"Quebecers know what they want, and what they want
is an independent Quebec in a strong Canada."
— Yvon Deschamps

§ A DEFT-NITION

An oxymoron is a rhetorical device in which contradictory or incongruous terms are conjoined so as to give point to the statement or expression. Examples are legal murder, bitter-sweet, cheerful pessimist, open secret, natural artifice, and the long-ago eviscerated Progressive Conservatives of Canadian politics. (Depending on your political perspective the term "compassionate conservative" can be seen as being redundant or oxymoronic.) Etymologically, the word oxymoron is itself oxymoronic deriving from the Greek words *oxys*, meaning "keen," and *moros*, meaning "foolish." Two other examples of oxymoron would be describing being trapped in a mine as "living death" and describing how a tsunami transformed an isle into a "hellish paradise." The term, however, is often erroneously used to refer to any contradiction in terms, often in an ironic sense, such as "criminal lawyer."

I suspect if you asked people to name one oxymoron, the most commonly received answer would be the half-baked *jumbo shrimp*. The term, oxymoron, is also often used cynically, or humorously, in many terms such as *military intelligence*, *good grief*, *good lawyer*, *peace offensive*, *business ethics*, *athletic scholarship*, and *Passover food*. If you are, like me, an uncool curmudgeon, and particularly dislike the non-melodious nature of hip-hop, you can include *hip-hop music* in the oxymoron category.

The oxymoron as wordplay is, not surprisingly, represented in literature. One sees its literary purpose in *Macbeth* in Act 2, Scene 3, when Macduff says to Macbeth, "I know this is a joyful trouble to you." Macbeth has just killed King Duncan but Macduff and others are not aware of the regicide. Macduff is telling Macbeth that while hosting the King is an imposition on Macbeth's household, it is also an opportunity for Macbeth to curry favour with Duncan. The irony of the "joyful trouble" oxymoron is that Macbeth has already offed the King. Similarly, we find these oxymorons (or oxymora) in Alexander Pope's poem *An Essay on*

Oxymoron

Criticism: "The bookful blockhead, ignorantly read, / With loads of learned lumber in his head." Here the pair of oxymorons "bookful blockhead" and "ignorantly read" point to the reality that though people may read a lot, this doesn't necessarily mean that they comprehend what they read, and therefore one shouldn't expect that they will exhibit enhanced understanding.

Not surprisingly, some of the great oxymorons have been penned by literary superstars. Chaucer gave us "hateful good"; Spenser, "proud humility"; Shakespeare, "sweet sorrow" and "cruel to be kind"; Milton, "darkness visible"; Pope, "damn with faint praise"; Thomson, "expressive silence"; Byron, "melancholy merriment"; Hemingway, "scalding coolness," and Tennyson, "falsely true." Tennyson's "falsely true" oxymoron is part of a two-line oxymoron trilogy from *Idylls of the King* which reads as follows:

> His honour rooted in dishonour stood,
> And faith unfaithful kept him falsely true.

The "sweet sorrow" oxymoron voiced by Juliet when she parts from Romeo is perhaps the most quoted oxymoron in the English language. Romeo, however, probably holds the Guinness record for most oxymorons in a short space when he confides to his friend Benvolio:

> Here's much to do with hate, but more with love.
> Why, then, O brawling love! O loving hate!
> O any thing, of nothing first create!
> O heavy lightness! serious vanity!
> Mis-shapen chaos of well-seeming forms!
> Feather of lead, bright smoke, cold fire, sick health!

Some other miscellaneous literary oxymorons include:

> So foul and fair a day I have not seen!
> — William Shakespeare, *Macbeth*, Act I, Scene III

> O miserable abundance, O beggarly riches!
> — John Donne, *Devotions on Emergent Occasions*

I do here make humbly bold to present them with a short account of themselves and their art. — Jonathan Swift

He was now sufficiently composed to order a funeral of modest magnificence. — Samuel Johnson

More recently, American novelist William Styron borrowed John Milton's "darkness visible" as the title of his book about his battle with depression. He characterized the term depression as a "wimp of a word" that doesn't convey the anguish and powerlessness of the sufferer. Substitutes like "melancholia," "blues" or "lowness" are not any more forceful. "Darkness visible" is an example of how an oxymoron can sometimes communicate an idea far better than an individual word.

✄ QUASI-OXYMORON PUZZLE

Use the following phrases to complete the oxymorons.

PHRASE		ANSWER
1	term for vampires	living _____
2	Schwarzenegger 1994 flick	True _____
3	fill-in for Letterman	guest _____
4	novel by Nabokov	Pale _____
5	use of condoms, e.g.	safe _____
6	Mafia attorneys	criminal _____
7	what the CIA provides	military _____
8	pacific overture	peace _____
9	ticketable way of braking	rolling _____
10	Charlie Brown's expression	good _____
11	boxer of 175 lbs.	light _____
12	Kubrick 1999 movie	Eyes _____
13	fairly hideous	pretty _____
14	jihad	holy _____
15	possible situation in Syria or Ukraine	civil _____
16	instructor in training	student _____
17	large seafood	jumbo _____

18	Drake's métier	rap	_____
19	thump by a professional wrestler	head	_____
20	2016 Oscar nominee	The Big	_____
21	bermudas	long	_____

ANSWERS: p. 145

Bermudas — Long Shorts.

So, words can be arranged in contradictory terms that make us think, and even smile at the resulting ideas. In the next chapter we will look at a very particular and personal form of arranged symmetry of words found occasionally in people's surnames with the intent of catching our attention and, sometimes, even amusing us.

CHAPTER 6

⅋

Aptronyms

"I do not like the man who squanders life for fame;
give me the man who living makes a name."
— Emily Dickinson

⅋ WHAT'S IN A LITERARY NAME?

What do the Dickensian character Ebenezer Scrooge, the Shakespearean character Mistress Quickly, and Richard Brinsley Sheridan's character Mrs. Malaprop have in common? The characters all have aptronyms. The *Oxford Companion to the English Language* defines an aptronym as a "name that matches its owner's occupation or character, often in a humorous or ironic way, such as *William Rumhole*, a London taverner." The word was coined in 1938 by American newspaper columnist Franklin P. Adams. He rearranged the first two letters of the word patronym, the naming from one's father, and arrived at the word "aptronym" which refers to an "apt" name.

English literature has brought us some memorable aptronyms. Not surprisingly, Shakespeare provides several, including Shallow, Quickly, Bottom, Falstaff and Toby Belch. John Bunyan gives us the very practical Mr. Worldly Wiseman and the desultory Mr. Talkative in *The Pilgrim's Progress*. Henry Fielding, in *Tom Jones*, presents us with righteous Squire Allworthy and in *Joseph Andrews* with the lascivious Lady Booby. And in his play *The Rivals*, Richard Brinsley Sheridan introduces Mrs. Malaprop (See Part II, Chapter 1) who is given to misapplications such as "an allegory on the banks of the Nile" (instead of an alligator).

Dr. Brain, Neuro-Surgeon.

Nineteenth-century writers in particular seemed to have enjoyed creating aptronymic characters. Thomas Hardy, in *Return of the Native*, named an impulsive character who conjures up the wild terrain of the heath, Wildeve; and Anthony Trollope unveils the (pre-Kevorkian) Dr. Fillgrave in his novel *Doctor Thorne*.

Charles Dickens, in particular, was a master of the literary aptronym. In *A Christmas Carol*, we find Scrooge, described as "squeezing, grasping . . . and hard as flint," as well as the be-wigged Old Fezziwig. *Oliver Twist* gives us the duo of the fussy official Bumble, and the burglar, Toby Crackit. In *Hard Times* we discover the austere Gradgrind and the pupil-hating M'Choakumchild, who teaches in Gradgrind's school. From *Dombey and Son*, we have the acid duet of Mrs. MacStinger and Susan Nipper. From *A Tale of Two Cities*, we find the Crunchers, a family of grave-robbers, and from *Martin Chuzzlewit*, the hypocritical Seth Pecksniff. In *David Copperfield*, we meet the villainous Murdstone, whose name suggests "murder," and in *Little Dorrit*, Mr. Merdle who is both a forger and a thief ("merde" being the French for excrement).

In the post-Dickensian era, the practice of naming literary characters based on their personality, was not overly popular. Of course, there were exceptions, such as Oscar Wilde's worthy Jack Worthing in *The Importance of Being Earnest* and Shaw's honest *Candida*. More recently, J.R.R. Tolkien in *Lord of the Rings* named Bilbo Baggins' mother Belladonna and presented the reader with the riddle of whether the name referenced her beauty or her poisonous nature.

James Joyce used aptronyms sublimely. His selection of the name Leopold Bloom as his protagonist in *Ulysses* is a study in irony. "Leopold" means a free man who is strong, yet "Bloom" refers to a fragile flower. Also, Bloom's real surname is Virag, but the name had been abandoned by his father. This name seems to be a play on virago, a word designating a war-like woman. Then we have Stephen Dedalus: "Stephen" means a crown and Stephen is the crown of his family with the burden of making a name for himself in Dublin society, even at the expense of his own siblings. Stephen is also the name of the first Christian martyr who was stoned by his peers for his radical beliefs. His surname Dedalus derives from the character in Greek mythology: Daedalus, a crafty architect who built an elaborate labyrinth for King Minos of Crete so that he could imprison his wife's monstrous son. Because of its complexity, Daedalus himself was barely able to escape it. Later, Daedalus builds wings for human flight and this leads to the death of his son Icarus. It would seem in *Ulysses* that Dedalus too wants to "fly away" from the constraints that politics and religion place on an artist.

If you are a fan of literary aptronyms, you'll be happy to know that they returned with a vengeance in the contemporary book world thanks to J.K. Rowling's *Harry Potter* series. Harry's nemesis is the evil Draco Malfoy. Here, both the first and last names describe his character. Draco is Latin for "dragon" and it was also the name of the "zero-tolerant" seventh-century B.C. Athenian lawmaker who lent his name to the word "draconian." *Mal foi* is French for "bad faith" and the name Malfoy conjures all sort of malicious and malignant actions. Malfoy belongs to the malevolent Slytherin House named after its founder Salazar Slytherin. "Slytherin" is a blend of the words "sly" and "slithering." Harry's supreme foe is Lord Voldemort. This name does double duty, for *vol de mort* in French means "flight from death" or "theft of death," and "vole" is also a type of rat-like rodent.

Most of Harry's teachers at Hogwarts wizardry school have evocative names. Professor Quirrel is both quarrelsome and squirrelly, and Professor Severus Snape is both severe and a cross between a snipe and a snake. Professor Alastor Moody waits many years for an opportunity to exact revenge, which is appropriate as *Alastor* in Greek means "avenging deity." Hogwarts professors tend to gravitate to fields which match their names. Vindictus Veridian teaches a class on curses and Professor Sprout's area of expertise is herbology. Professor Remus Lupin teaches a course "Defense Against the Dark Arts." Guess what he turns out to be? Those who know Latin and Roman mythology will be able to divine that he is doubly a werewolf. According to lore, Remus, the co-founder of Rome, was suckled by a wolf, and *lupus* is the Latin word for "wolf."

Apart from her character aptronyms, Rowling is also adept at creating suggestive place names. The author, who was born in Chipping Sodbury, near Bristol, in England, has said that the peculiar sound of her birthplace may have contributed to her love for curious-sounding words in later life. Harry's highly obnoxious adoptive family, the Dursleys, live in Little Whinging ("whingeing" is the British English equivalent to "whining"). Harry's "porky" cousin Dudley Dursley attends Smelting School ("smelt" is the British English past tense of "smell"). Rowling, however, has particular fun with the two shopping streets that wizards frequent in London. One is called Diagon Alley, an obvious pun on "diagonally," as one can't just walk straight into Diagon Alley but must seemingly enter "diagonally." The other street she calls "Knockturn Alley," a play on the word "nocturnally."

Karl Jung, in *Synchronicity*, alluded to the possibility that there may be a suggestive effect to names (after all, many surnames, such as Archer and Weaver, derived originally from a person's occupation). In 1994, the British magazine *New Scientist* went somewhat further. It posited the (I believe specious) argument that people actually gravitate towards jobs that reflect their surnames. They called this process "nominative determinism" and suggested that there is a subconscious imperative that impels one to find a job that fits one's surname. Readers were asked to supply examples of this process and, as a result, *New Scientist* was inundated with hundreds of "proofs." In 1998, *New Scientist* resurrected the controversy when they quoted the following underwhelming statement in Lawrence Casler's article "Put the Blame on Name" that appeared in the journal *Psychological Reports* in 1975: "There is a determinant whose effect may not be phenomenal but is probably more than nominal, namely the name."

As examples of nominative determinism, *New Scientist* listed John Barnacle's decision to become a marine-timber expert, and the vocation of Daniel Snowman who wrote the book *Pole Positions: The Polar Regions and the Future of the Planet*. Also cited were Britain's Meteorological Office which features staff with the surnames Flood, Frost, Thundercliffe and Weatherall, and the U.S. National Weather Service employee Dave Storm. As a proud Montrealer, I was saddened that my hometown received short shrift in the *New Scientist* list of aptronyms. It didn't reference McGill's ornithology professor David Bird who wrote a column about birds in the *Gazette* for twenty-eight years. Also ignored were ill-fated Will Drop, a local window cleaner who died in a fall, and one-time Director of Pediatric Urology at the Montreal Children's Hospital, Joao Luiz Pippi-Salle.

It would appear that academics in particular follow this onomastic imperative. For example, University of Minnesota biology professor David Hoppe is an expert on deformed frogs; professor of psychiatry Jules Angst has published works about anxiety; and Peter Skidmore was a researcher into cow dung ecology. As karma would have it, astronomy buffs are guided not by the stars but by their names. To wit, we have professor of theoretical physics Alan Heavens, astronomy professor Charles Telesco, astronomer Summer Starrfield, not to mention astronaut Sally Ride.

Probably due to some quantum dynamic process I'm not bright enough to fathom, nominative determinism sometimes works in reverse. While Wikipedia lists an American rabbi named Alexander D. Goode, this is countered by Cardinal Jaime Sin, Archbishop of Manila, who passed away in 2005. There are also the following "inaptronyms": David Soberman, who worked in marketing for Dow Breweries; dentists Emily Payne and Keith Au (pronounced "ow"); police chiefs Clayton Crooke and Ken Lawless; the British building company R. Crumbleholme & Son; the psychiatry professor William C. Dement; and finally Henry Calamity who, in March 1969, was voted the Santa Fe Railroad's "safety man of the month."

Hmm! After looking at all these examples, I begin to wonder if perhaps there is something to this nominative determinism process. After all, Toronto mayor John Tory was the former leader of the Tories in Ontario; Martin Short is short; the world's fastest man Usain Bolt does bolt out of the blocks; former U.S. Congressman Tom DeLay was prone to filibuster and American Jacques P. Moron sold drugs to narcs. Just in case you're not convinced by all this "evidence" take note that on October 6, 1941, the unfortunate duo of Wilburn and Frizzel were subjected to the electric chair at Florida State Prison. The mind boggles as the body smoulders.

Clearly, people like to manipulate words as names as both a serious and humorous means of finding significance, feigned or not. In the next chapter, the arrangement of letters provides the wit, and while the acronymic origins of words such as radar (radio detection and ranging) are oft forgotten, we will see that wags like to attribute acronymic origins for pure whimsy.

CHAPTER 7

ℬ

Tongue-in-Cheek Acronyms

"Acronyms are your allies. They sound impressive
while conveying no information. Use them liberally."
— Scott Adams

ℬ WHY ACRONYMS?

Take the following two sentences: i) "By taking AZT, the HIV patient forestalled getting AIDS and no DNA changes occurred." ii) "Despite being exposed to DDT and LSD, his level of ACTH didn't drop." In the first sentence, having to employ the words "azido thymidine," "human-immuno-deficiency virus," and "acquired immune deficiency syndrome" as well as "deoxyribonucleic acid" would have resulted in a sentence more than twice as long. And notwithstanding that the second sentence probably doesn't make medical sense, at least by using acronyms instead of the words "dichlorodiphenyl-trichloroethane," "lysergic acid diethyl-amine" and "adrenocorticotropic hormone," the gibberish has been reduced by 57.4%.

The word "acronym" is of relatively young vintage. It marries the prefix *acr-* meaning outer end or tip (from the Greek *akros*), along with the *-onym* suffix, meaning name, and is found in words such as homonym and synonym. The first citation of the word is in 1943 and there is little evidence that words were created in this fashion before the twentieth century. John Ayto, in *Twentieth Century Words*, speculates that "the proliferation of polynomial governmental agencies, international organizations, and military units as the century has progressed (the last particularly during World War II) has contributed significantly to its growth."

We also see acronyms increasingly used to describe different types of people, often not in a particularly complimentary fashion. Observe "WASP," White Anglo-Saxon Protestant; "yuppie," young urban professional (+ *-ie* suffix); "woopie," well-off older person (+ *-ie* suffix); "dink," double income no kids; "dwem," dead white European male; "posslq," person of opposite sex sharing living quarters, and "bobo," bourgeois bohemian. Some of these have even spawned subgroups. For example, the first letter of "buppie" refers to "black" urban professional.

Keep it simple, stupid.

I suppose that short of cracking a code, making one up is a favourite pastime of many a language fiend. Using acronyms as the building block of the code has been the preferred construction material of many a wag. Acronyms are a time-saving means of disparagement. While growing up, my hard-working father enlightened me that PhD really stood for "papa has dough." Applying the same logic to the dialect of acronyms, the legal degree LLD becomes "license to lie damnably"; MBA graduates to "mediocre but arrogant"; TLC degenerates into "total lack of concern"; CIA subverts into "caught in the act"; NATO reshapes to "no action, talk only"; MAFIA turns into "mother and father Italian association"; and OPEC breaks down to "oil people ending competition."

Cars have also been a pet target of acronymic satire. In alphabetic order, the cabalistic meaning of various automobiles is revealed as:

ACURA — Asia's curse upon rural America

AUDI — another useless damn import

BMW — big money waste (in Quebec it would be bus, metro, walk — as "metro" is the French word for subway)

CHEVROLET — can hear every valve rattle on long extended trips

FIAT — fix it again, Tony (it actually stands for Fabbrica Italiana Automobili Torino)

FORD — fix or repair daily

HYUNDAI — hope you understand nothing's driveable and inexpensive

PORSCHE — proof of rich spoiled children having everything

VOLVO — very odd-looking vehicular object

Airlines do not escape the target of acronymic wrath. Observe, ALITALIA, "always late in takeoffs and landings in airport"; AMERICAN, "a miracle each rider is currently alive now"; DELTA, "doesn't ever leave the airport"; EL AL, "embarks late, arrives late"; and erstwhile SABENA, "such a bad experience, never again" (in fact, Societé Anonyme Belge d'Exploitation de la Navigation Aérienne).

Nowadays, however, acronyms are probably most prevalent in the field of computers. We are assailed by countless examples such as CD-ROM, "compact disc-read only memory"; MIPS, "millions of instructions per second," and WYSIWYG, "what you see is what you get," an acronym used to describe a system in which content during editing appears very similar to the final product.

Lately, bogus computer acronyms have supplanted car acronyms as the favourite forum for waggish wordsmiths. COMPUTER, itself, is said to stand for "capable of making perfectly uncomplicated tasks extremely rigorous."

Here's more of this type of witty crypto-cyber-sampling:

> FACEBOOK — friends are compulsively elicited by obnoxious online knuckleheads
>
> IBM — I blame Microsoft
>
> MICROSOFT — most intelligent customers realize our software only fools teenagers
>
> TWITTER — the world is trying to eradicate reading
>
> WINDOWS — will install needless data on whole system

✂ REAL ACRONYM PUZZLE

Do you know what these alphabetically-ordered acronyms stand for?

ACRONYM	ANSWER
1 AWOL	__________
2 BRIC	__________
3 CAD/CAM	__________
4 DOS	__________
5 Epcot	__________

6　fubar　　　　　　　　_____

7　guppie　　　　　　　_____

8　hazmat　　　　　　　_____

9　IKEA　　　　　　　　_____

10　JAG　　　　　　　　_____

11　kiss　　　　　　　　_____

12　laser　　　　　　　　_____

13　MADD　　　　　　　_____

14　nimby　　　　　　　_____

15　OCD　　　　　　　　_____

16　PETA　　　　　　　　_____

17　quasar　　　　　　　_____

18　radar　　　　　　　　_____

19　snafu　　　　　　　　_____

20　TGIF　　　　　　　　_____

21　UNICEF*　　　　　　_____

22　VCR　　　　　　　　_____

23　WHO　　　　　　　　_____

24　XL　　　　　　　　　_____

25　yolo　　　　　　　　_____

26　zip　　　　　　　　　_____

* *Hint: It doesn't stand for underage nocturnal imps clutching extorted funds.*

ANSWERS: p. 146

Whether you are devout or a truth-seeker, if you are confused by acronyms, and see them as mere clusters of letters, you are bound to find the subject matter of the next chapter, riddles, an even greater enigma, notwithstanding the fact that this form of wordplay was often used to educate children.

CHAPTER 8

%

Riddles

Riddle-me, riddle-me, riddle-me-ree,
Perhaps you can tell what this riddle may be:
As deep as a house, as round as a cup,
And all the King's horses can't draw it up.

Answer: Well

— Edward D. Nudelman,
The Jessie Willcox Smith Mother Goose (1914)

% ARE RIDDLES JUST KIDS' STUFF?

Peter Farb, in *Word Play*, relates that "the majority of children are strikingly punctual in acquiring a repertory of riddles at about six or seven, and at that age they will tell about three times as many joking riddles as jokes in any other form. During the next several years, riddles continue to make up about a half of a child's store of jokes, and it is not until about the age of eleven that they are discarded in favor of anecdotes."

According to Farb, "instead of offering children . . . specific instructions for day-to-day living, riddles are a more subtle education for life in general. They are stepping stones to adulthood because they prepare the child for an important aspect of life in all culture's interrogation. . . . Apparently the riddle affords excellent preparation for the role which speakers will assume as adults in their speech communities."

Unfortunately, most adults do not seem to enjoy riddles unless they are camouflaged within a detective story or in a mathematical enigma. So, in our society, riddles are mainly the preserve of children, but truth be told, they rank with fables, folk tales, myths and proverbs as one of the most widespread forms of thought. Essentially, riddles are metaphors, and metaphors are the result of connections between seemingly disparate objects. In *Riddle Me This*, author Phil Cousineau states, "part of the genius of riddles is the way they illustrate the perennial wisdom that things aren't always what they seem, and the manner in which they reveal the 'genius,' the vital life, in everything."

The word riddle derives from the Old English *raedal* meaning "to counsel" which is also the origin of the verb "to read." The oldest collection of riddles is found in the eighth-century Old English *Exeter Book* which posed ninety-five riddles in poetic form. Here is a modern translation of one of them:

A moth ate words. To me it seemed
a remarkable fate, when I learned of the marvel,
that the worm had swallowed the speech of a man,
a thief in the night, a renowned saying
and its place itself. Though he swallowed the word
the thieving stranger was no whit the wiser.

Answer: Bookworm

Riddles were perhaps the most common way in which supernatural forces were believed to communicate with mere mortals, and as such their mediums were priests, oracles and soothsayers. Until well into the Renaissance, anagrams (a word re-arranged to form a different word) were thought to be messages from the gods affecting a person's fate. I suppose somebody divined at that juncture that a funeral didn't mean "real fun."

So notwithstanding its association with mere whimsy, the riddle has a hallowed place in many religions. For example, in the Biblical book of *Judges*, Samson offers this conundrum: "Out of the eater came something to eat; Out of the strong came something sweet." Delilah uses her charms to worm the answer from her main squeeze: he had seen a swarm of bees making honey in the carcass of a lion. Later in the Bible, it is related in I Kings 10: "when the queen of Sheba heard of the fame of Solomon . . . she came to prove him with hard questions. . . . And Solomon told [answered] her all her questions: there was not any thing hid from the king." King Solomon and King Hiram of Tyre were known to have organized riddling contests merely for their entertainment value and to challenge the mental agility of contestants.

Riddles are also used as a form of teaching in religious texts such as the Haggadah, which is read at Passover Seders. That riddles should be featured in religious texts is not surprising. After all, the riddle of who we are and why we are here is omnipresent, and in trying to solve riddles, one is, in a sense, trying to find the meaning of life. Brahmin priests posed riddles in the sacred pages of the Rig Veda, and Mohammed did likewise in the Koran. In Zen Buddhism, koans are enigmatic stories or questions given to students by their teachers to test their understanding of Zen.

In many ancient riddle contests, the penalty for losing the contest was the forfeiture of your life — hardly child's play. J.R.R. Tolkien, in *The Hobbit*, highlights this tradition in the chapter entitled "Riddles in the Dark" where Gollum and Bilbo try to guess each other's riddles in a life-and-death battle of wits. Similarly, Oedipus, while on his way to Thebes, encounters the Sphinx and stakes his life on solving the riddle of the Sphinx: "What walks on four legs in the morning, two legs at noon, and three legs in the evening?" Oedipus figures out this complex conundrum — Man. He crawls as an infant, walks upright as an adult, and uses a staff in old age. Oedipus thus destroys the Sphinx and is proclaimed the King of Thebes. Along with the throne, he is rewarded with the royal widow Jocasta, who turns out to be his mother. This eventually destroys Oedipus but continues to delight psychiatrists two millennia hence.

Furthermore, riddles played an important role in ancient life-cycle rituals, such as weddings and funerals. J. G. Frazer relates in *The Golden*

Bough that "In Brittany, after a burial, when the rest have gone to partake of the funeral banquet, old men remain behind in the graveyard and . . . ask each other riddles." From the same source, we learn about the elaborate rain-making ceremonies of the Ba-Thonga, a Bantu tribe: "Gesticulating wildly, naked women would sing 'Rain, fall.' If any man was to approach the women, they would beat him and put riddles to him which he would have to answer in the most filthy language borrowed from the circumcision ceremonies; for obscene words, which are usually forbidden, are customary and legitimate on certain occasions."

Riddles could also be used to bring out the ambiguities of an individual's life, especially if the person was deemed to be untrustworthy, as in this 1647 epitaph on the Earl of Strafford by the witty John Cleveland:

> Here lies wise and valiant dust,
> Huddled up 'twixt fit and just:
> Strafford, who was hurried hence
> 'Twixt treason and convenience.
> He spent his time here in a mist,
> A Papist, yet a Calvinist...
> Riddles lie here, or in a word,
> Here lies blood; and let it lie
> Speechless still, and never cry.

Riddles were popular with other ethnicities. In 1783, the Finnish scholar Christfrid Ganander wrote of the tradition of the Goths: "Our ancestors in the kingdom tested with riddles the acuity, intelligence and skills of each other. . . . Also when a suitor . . . came to ask for a girl . . . riddles were posed to him . . . and if he could answer and interpret them, he received the girl, otherwise not, but was classified as stupid and good for nothing."

Special riddling banquets were organized by the ancient Greeks to entertain guests. In fact, Aesop's fables are narrative riddles themselves. The Romans featured riddles in the Saturnalia (Dec. 17–23, over the winter solstice). The popularity of riddles grew in the later Roman Empire, and collections of riddles were published. Perhaps the most famous of these was by Symphosius. Here is one of his riddles:

Unlike my mother, in semblance different from my
father, of mingled race, a breed unfit for progeny,
of others am I born, and none is born of me.

Answer: Mule

Surprisingly, a somewhat naughty fourteenth-century Benedictine monk named Claret published a collection of 136 riddles that exploited sexual double entendres, creating lascivious images in the mind of the puzzle solver. Here is an example:

A vessel have I, That is round like a pear,
Moist in the middle, Surrounded with hair;
And often it happens, That water flows there.

Answer: Eye

Riddles became extremely popular in the eighteenth century and many newspapers and magazines featured riddles that readers were implored to solve. Many of the most distinguished members of the literati composed these riddles as a proof of their literary skill. American inventor Benjamin Franklin constructed many riddles under the name of Richard Saunders, and these were included in his 1732 book *Poor Richard's Almanack*.

So popular did riddles become at this time that a demand for variety arose. This led to the invention of the "charade." It arrived in America through the *Penny Post*, a magazine first published in 1769. Charades are solved one syllable, word, or line at a time by unravelling the double meanings suggested by the individual syllables, words or lines, as in the following:

My first is to ramble; my next is to retreat;
My whole oft enrages in summer's fierce heat.
Who am I?

Answer: Gadfly

The first part of the first line provides a clue to the first syllable of the answer (to gad is to go), and the second part of the first line provides a clue as to the second syllable of the answer (to retreat is to fly). The second line completes the description of the whole object (a gadfly being a kind of horsefly, although today we more often think of a critical person who provokes a response in others).

In the nineteenth century, charades developed into "mime charades" which became a popular parlour game. Mime charades were played by teams who acted out the syllables of a word, a complete word, or a phrase in pantomime. For example, if the answer to the charade is *The King's Speech* the team would try to mime the words "king" and "speech." Mime charades often used elaborate costumes, and at times were risqué in nature. Aficionados of William Thackeray's *Vanity Fair* might recall the scene where the indomitable Becky Sharp plays the part of the femme fatale Clytemnestra with such "ghastly truth" that she left her audience speechless with a mixture of horror and awe.

Also in the nineteenth century, two ancient riddle genres that had been revived in the seventeenth century became extremely popular. The first of these riddle genres is "conundrums" — riddles that use the similar sounds of word pairs such as "blue" and "blew," and the different meanings of phrases such as "all over."

Another ancient riddle genre that was revived in the seventeenth century and regained popularity in Victorian England was the "enigma," rhyming riddles that contain one or more veiled references to the answer. Here follows a famous enigma composed by the British statesman George Canning:

> A word there is of plural number,
> Foe to ease and tranquil slumber,
> Any other word you take,
> And add an "s" will plural make,
> But if you add an "s" to this,
> So strange the metamorphosis;
> Plural is plural now no more
> And sweet what bitter was before.

Answer: Cares/Caress

Iona and Peter Opie compiled riddles from British children in the 1950s. In their book, *The Lore and Language of Schoolchildren*, they relate that many of the riddles submitted were centuries old. Two such riddles are found in *Demaundes Joyous* printed in 1511 in London: i) *"How deep is the ocean?"* Answer: A stone's throw, and ii) *"How many balls of string would it take to reach the moon?"* Answer: One, if it was long enough.

How many balls of string would it take to reach the moon?

By the turn of the twentieth century, most young children would have giggled at the obviousness of many riddles such as the following, which had been repeated for countless generations:

I have an apple I can't cut,
A blanket I can't fold,
And so much money I can't count it.

Answer: Sun, Sky, Stars

World authority on riddles, Archer Taylor, says that riddles "describe objects in intentionally misleading terms. Humpty Dumpty tells of a man who rolls, falls and is injured beyond being put together again. This description is true enough but has nothing to do with the use of an egg. A child of ten . . . sees objects in this way and enjoys and remembers them. An adult no longer sees them in this way and no longer remembers riddles."

So, what is the function of riddles? Aside from the joy and challenges they impart to participants, riddles inform us that there is no direct link between language and reality, and, to paraphrase the Bard, that what appears to be foul may indeed be fair, and fair may really be foul. Riddles help us understand that the world is replete with delightful metaphors and enlightening ambiguity. Their capacity for multiple solutions alerts us to the reality that reductionist solutions are facile and usually only tell a fragment of a story. On a practical level, they might remind someone entering into a contractual agreement that words are merely a symbol of reality.

RIDDLE PUZZLE

As an author and columnist writing about the variations and complexities of the English language, I'm invited to many elementary and secondary schools to speak to students about the joys of language. In my presentations, I usually include the following list of riddles, and most times at least one person in the class knows, or can figure out the answer. See how many of these you can answer:

QUESTION	ANSWER
1 What goes up but never comes down?	_____
2 What can you catch but can't throw?	_____
3 What belongs to you, but others use it more than you do?	_____
4 What is black and white and red all over?	_____
5 What has four wheels and flies?	_____
6 What can go around the world but stays in a corner?	_____
7 What gets wetter and wetter the more it dries?	_____
8 What is the difference between a hill and a pill?	_____
9 I'm light as a feather but nobody can hold me for more than several minutes?	_____
10 Give me food and I'll live; give me water and I'll die. What am I?	_____
11 Name me and you destroy me. What am I?	_____
12 What can run but never walks, has a mouth but never talks, has a head but never weeps, has a bed but never sleeps?	_____
13 You throw away the outside and cook the inside, then you eat the outside and throw away the inside. What is it?	_____
14 I am weightless but you can see me, put me in a bucket and I'll make it lighter. What am I?	_____
15 What goes up and down the stairs without moving?	_____
16 If you're an American outside of the bathroom, what are you in the bathroom?	_____

17 There was a green house. Inside the green house there was a white house. Inside the white house there was a red house. Inside the red house there were lots of babies. What is it? _____

18 I never was, am always to be. No one ever saw me, nor ever will. Yet I am the confidence of all, to live and breathe on this terrestrial ball. What am I? _____

19 The one who makes it, sells it. The one who buys it, never uses it. The one who uses it never knows that he's using it. What is it? _____

20 What's black when you get it, red when you use it, and white when you're all through with it? _____

21 I'm where yesterday follows today and tomorrow is in the middle. What am I? _____

ANSWERS: p. 147

Riddles are an example of the multifaceted nature of language as they entertain us and hopefully elicit some wisdom. In the next chapter we will look at how we manipulate language to achieve superiority, albeit often in a humorous way, in our daily attempt at one-upmanship over our rivals.

CHAPTER 9

§

Creative Insults

"There's no possibility of being witty without
a little ill-nature; the malice of a good thing
is the barb that makes it stick."
— Richard Brinsley Sheridan, *The School For Scandal*

§ SLINGS AND ARROWS

When I saw Shakespeare's *The Tempest* some years ago at the Stratford
Festival in Stratford, Ontario, I was struck once again by this line from
Caliban, "You taught me language; and my profit on't is, I know how to
curse." I will leave it to Shakespearean scholars to decide whether the
Bard's freckled monster was pleased or displeased with his powers of
execration, but I, for one, see much profit in invective. Let's face it. Given
that many people behave abominably, a good insult is definitely required
by both individuals and society at large. As Somerset Maugham said
slyly in *The Moon and Six Pence*, "Impropriety is the soul of wit." Freud
believed that verbal wit serves as a safe outlet for repressed impulses.

Further, if one's aggression is likely to cause retaliation, it is prudent that the slings and arrows be linguistic rather than physical.

In his book *The Lost Art of Profanity*, written in 1948, Burges Johnson laments that "the vocabulary of vituperation is today a poverty-stricken one," and lists some of the sublime insults to be found in the works of literary lights such as Chaucer, Shakespeare, Milton and Pope. While it is true that the modern language of denigration is highly unimaginative and dominated particularly by the F-word and nether parts of the anatomy, I believe Johnson was being unduly pessimistic in his analysis.

All is not lost. I culled through my collection of books of quotations and I dug up some more recent vituperative pearls. Not surprisingly, many come from the world of politics. When required, I have revealed the victim of the venom:

> David Lloyd George could not see a belt without hitting below it. — Margot Asquith

> I only wish I knew him [Bill Vander Zalm] before his lobotomy. — Kim Campbell

> Clement Attlee is a modest man, who has a good deal to be modest about. — Winston Churchill

> He [Stafford Cripps] has all the virtues I dislike and none of the vices I admire. — Winston Churchill

> He [William Gladstone] is a sophisticated rhetorician, inebriated with the exuberance of his verbosity. — Benjamin Disraeli

> His [Ronald Reagan's] ignorance is encyclopedic. — Abba Eban

> In a disastrous fire in President Reagan's library both books were burned. And the tragedy is he hadn't finished coloring one. — Jonathan Hunt

> He [Gerald Ford] is so dumb he can't fart and chew gum at the same time — Lyndon Baines Johnson (the sanitized version has it as "can't walk and . . .")

He [possibly, Stephen Douglas] compresses the most words into the smallest idea of any man I know. — Abraham Lincoln

When they circumcised Herbert Samuel they threw away the wrong bit. — David Lloyd George

Since in politics, it takes at least "two to tangle," we have the following verbal sparring:

LABOUR MP BESSIE BRADDOCK: Winston, you're drunk.
WINSTON CHURCHILL: Bessie, you're ugly. But tomorrow I shall be sober.

NANCY ASTOR: If I were your wife I would put poison in your coffee.
WINSTON CHURCHILL: And if I were your husband I would drink it.

WILLIAM GLADSTONE: You sir, shall either die of hanging, or from a social disease.
BENJAMIN DISRAELI: That all depends, sir, whether I embrace your politics or your mistress. (Some sources show that this exchange originated with the Earl of Sandwich and John Wilkes.)

AUSTRALIAN PM PAUL KEATING: John Hewson is simply a shiver looking for a spine to run up.
KEATING'S POLITICAL FOE JOHN HEWSON: I decided the worst thing you can call Paul Keating, quite frankly, is Paul Keating.

Occasionally, non-politicians enter the caustic arena:

His lack of education is more than compensated for by his keen moral bankruptcy. — Woody Allen

Of course, we all know that Morris was a wonderful all-round man, but the act of walking around him always tired me. — Max Beerbohm

I feel so miserable without you; it's almost like having you here. — Stephen Bishop

He is a self-made man and worships his creator. — John Bright

He hasn't an enemy in the world, but all his friends hate him. — Eddie Cantor

There are some people who leave the impression not so lasting as the impact of an oar upon the water. — Kate Chopin

I've just learned about his illness. Let's hope it's nothing trivial. — Irvin S. Cobb

His wit invites you by his looks to come, but when you knock it never is at home. — William Cowper

I have never killed a man, but I have read many obituaries with great pleasure. — Clarence Darrow

He [Ernest Hemingway] has never been known to use a word that might send a reader to the dictionary. — William Faulkner

He is not only dull himself but the cause of dullness in others. — Samuel Foote

No one can have a higher opinion of him than I have, and I think he's a dirty little beast. — W. S. Gilbert

We all have inferiority complexes of various sizes. But yours [Arthur Koestler] isn't a complex, it's a cathedral. — Editor Otto Katz

He had delusions of adequacy. — Walter Kerr

Sometimes when you look into his eyes you get the feeling that someone else is driving. — David Letterman

I've had a perfectly wonderful evening. But this wasn't it.
— Groucho Marx

He is one of the people who would be enormously improved by death. — H. H. Munro

I didn't attend the funeral, but I sent a nice letter saying I approved of it. — Mark Twain

His mother should have thrown him away and kept the stork. — Mae West

You have Van Gogh's ear for music. — Billy Wilder

He loves nature in spite of what it did to him. — Forrest Tucker

Now there goes a man with an open mind. You can feel the draft from here. — Groucho Marx

Now there goes a man with an open mind.

Clearly, verbal jousting transcends politics, although a politician may be involved, as in these two quips featuring George Bernard Shaw and Winston Churchill outside the political arena:

> The celebrated dancer Isadora Duncan once wrote to George Bernard Shaw declaring that, given the principles of eugenics, they should have a child together. "Think of it!" she enthused. "With my body and your brains, what a wonder it would be." "Yes," Shaw replied. "But what if it had my body and your brains?"

> In a note to Winston Churchill, George Bernard Shaw wrote: "I am enclosing two tickets to the first night of my new play; bring a friend . . . if you have one." In reply, Churchill responded: "Cannot possibly attend first night, will attend second, if there is one."

⍦ THE BARD'S BARBS

No one, however, holds a candle to William Shakespeare when it comes to creative put-downs. Here is a soupçon of his vituperative gems:

> His brain is as dry as the remaining biscuit after voyage.
> — *As You Like It*

> [You are] one that converses more with the buttock of the night than with the forehead of the morning.
> — *Coriolanus*

> There is no more mercy in him than there is milk in a male tiger. — *Coriolanus*

> It is fit I should commit offence to my inferiors.
> — *Cymbeline*

> God has given you one face and you make yourself another. — *Hamlet*

> What is this quintessence of dust? — *Hamlet*

You're a wretch whose natural gifts were poor. — *Hamlet*

Thou art essentially a natural coward without instinct.
— *Henry IV, Part I*

A man made after supper of a cheese-paring.
— *Henry IV, Part 2*

Kate, whose face is not worth sunburning . . . — *Henry V*

Sell your face for five pence and 'tis dear. — *King Lear*

Thou whoreson zed! Thou unnecessary letter! — *King Lear*

Ay if a' have no more blood in's belly than will sup a flea.
— *Love's Labour's Lost*

[You are] an index and prologue to the history of lust
and foul thoughts. — *Othello*

Ajax, that wears his brain on his belly and his guts in
his head. He hath not so much brain as earwax.
— *Troilus and Cressida*

Some of the finest of Shakespeare's barbs are to be found in quarrels
between young people who are in the process of falling in love, although
they don't know it at the time:

BEATRICE: I wonder that you will still be talking, Signor
Benedick. Nobody marks you.

BENEDICK: What! My dear Lady Disdain, are you yet
living? — *Much Ado About Nothing*

✤ CHIASTIC INSULTS

A sub-genre of insult involves the literary device, chiasmus, which is defined by *The Concise Oxford Dictionary of Literary Terms* as "a figure of
speech by which the order of the terms in the first of two parallel clauses

is reversed in the second." This may involve a repetition of the same words, such as "Pleasure's a sin, and sometimes sin's a pleasure," uttered by a hedonistic Lord Byron, or just a reversed parallel between two corresponding pairs of ideas.

According to the *OED* the term "chiasmus" made its first published English appearance in 1871, when a British scholar named A. S. Wilkins wrote about an observation from Cicero: "This a good instance of the . . . figure called chiasmus. . . ." "Chiasmus" (pronounced kye-AZ-muss) is named after the Greek letter *chi* (Χ), indicating a "criss-cross" arrangement of terms.

One can literally mark many chiastic expressions with an *x*. Take Mae West's famous quip:

"It's not the *men* in my *life*

It's the *life* in my *men*."

Not surprisingly, the Bard of Avon was master of chiasmus. Here is a small sample of Shakespeare's chiastic vituperations:

Better a witty fool than a foolish wit. — *Twelfth Night*

O powerful love, that in some respects makes a beast a man, in some other, a man a beast. — *The Merry Wives of Windsor*

That one for all, or all for one we gage. — *The Rape of Lucrece*

I wasted time, and now doth time waste me. — *King Richard II*

CHIEF JUSTICE: Your means are very slender, and your waste is great.
FALSTAFF: I would it were otherwise. I would my means were greater and my waist slenderer. — *King Henry IV, Part II*

Humour is often created by establishing incongruity, and chiasmus performs this function, especially with implied statements. Among non-Shakespearian users of chiasmus, Oscar Wilde was a master with this type of transposition. A few of his classics are as follows:

> Work is the curse of the drinking class (parodying
> "drink is the curse of the working class").

> Life imitates art far more than art imitates life.

> The English have a miraculous power of turning
> wine into water.

Of course, chiasmus is not only used for put-downs; it can also be used in a positive manner, as evidenced in JFK's famous plea: "Ask not what your country can do for you, ask what you can do for your country." Chiasmus can even be used to submit a compliment, as in this quip from Queen Elizabeth I to Sir Walter Raleigh after he introduced tobacco into England: "I have seen many a man turn his gold into smoke, but you are the first who has turned smoke into gold."

I particularly enjoy the wordplay when this genre serves as obloquy. Here are some of my favourite examples:

> Pope Alexander VI, who was on St. Peter's throne from
> 1492 to 1503, fathered Cesare Borgia who gained infamy as
> an adult both as a soldier and a ruler. Not surprisingly, both
> father and son elicited the poison pens of some Protestant
> commentators. In 1632 Dutch writer Jacob Cat opined, "It
> was said of Pope Alexandre VI and of his son . . . that the
> father never did what he said, and the son never said what
> he did."

> Lexicographer Samuel Johnson told an aspiring writer,
> "Your manuscript is both good and original: but the part
> that is good is not original, and the part that is original
> is not good."

Johnson, on another occasion, said, "This man (Lord Chesterfield) I thought had been a lord among wits; but, I find, he is only a wit among Lords."

In *The Dunciad*, Alexander Pope wrote of a would-be wit: "A wit with dunces, and a dunce with wits."

When John F. Kennedy ran for the American presidency, a group of Protestant ministers led by Norman Vincent Peale issued a statement opposing the candidature of a Catholic. This position led Kennedy's fellow Democrat Adlai Stevenson to quip that, "I find (Saint) Paul appealing and Peale appalling."

Commenting on the writing style of Henry James, Mrs. Henry Adams observed, "It's not that he 'bites off more than he can chew' . . . but he chews more than he bites off."

And whenever you feel that life is inherently unfair, remember this chiastic maxim by Groucho Marx: "Time wounds all heels."

❧ YIDDISH CURSING — OY VEY!

Cursing has proved to be a cathartic tool for many oppressed minorities, a truth borne out by the colourful curses to be found among chronically subjugated groups such as gypsies, African-Americans and, of course, Eastern European Jews.

The Jews who lived in Eastern Europe before WWII had no problems cursing creatively, as they enjoyed the advantage of speaking Yiddish, a tongue seemingly fashioned exclusively for the prickly barb. Yiddish curses should not be confused with the Hebraic curses of the Bible. Hebrew curses were deadly serious, whereas there is a humorous thrust to almost all Yiddish curses. Although most people associate cursing with malevolence, Yiddish ones can be downright jocular. This is because the Yiddish curser usually does not believe in the power of his or her execrations. Leo Rosten, author of *Joys of Yiddish*, described the dialect as "a tongue that never takes its tongue out of its cheek."

Yiddish cursing developed into a choreographed activity where satisfaction was gained by ejaculating an imaginative curse. Many of the curses were improvised and were designed to exhibit the verbal nimbleness of the execrator. This is not to say that ill will was never directed towards others in Yiddish curses. Shtetl life in Eastern Europe was onerous, and interactions did not take place in idyllically bucolic settings with fiddlers prancing on rooftops. In this environment, an acerbic wit and a good delivery could earn one much respect. Moreover, in cursing your neighbour or your competitor at the market, you could imagine that the object of your scorn was the Czar or some other oppressor, and receive a sense of satisfaction from this thought.

Yiddish curses lull you in the beginning with their seeming innocence, then flatten you with the punch line. Excellent examples of this verbal feinting include the following: "May you lose all your teeth except one — so you can have a tooth ache," and "May you fall into the outhouse just as a regiment of Cossacks finishes a prune stew and twelve barrels of beer!"

Yiddish cursing was, by and large, the domain of women. The men enjoyed sanctuary in holy studies, but Jewish women could not indulge in this escape. Because men devoted most of their time to religious study, women became the family providers. The only profession open to them was work at the market, and to release anxiety in this hectic workplace, it was necessary to learn to "curse like a market-woman."

One would never merely say "Drop dead!" in Yiddish. The simplest way of expressing this aspiration was "Into the earth with you!" or "May he grow like an onion — with his head in the ground." Since a child could only be named after a deceased person, you could kill with kindness by saying "May they name a baby after you!" Wishing an adversary's death could also be couched in other such blessings, as in "May you have a sweet death and have a wagonload of sugar run over you"; or in "May God bless you with a son so smart he learns the mourner's prayer before his Bar Mitzvah speech!" and the saccharine "May you be spared the indignities of old age!"

Wishing disease or pain on someone was a popular theme, especially if the individual was wealthy. Benedictions took sudden U-turns and mu-

May you feast on chopped liver with onions, chicken soup with matzah balls, brisket with gravy and latkes and may it all be contaminated with E. coli.

tated into maledictions, such as "May he own ten shiploads of gold and may all of it be spent on sickness." Many of these ill-wishes of disease featured cholera, such as: "May the cholera seize him," "A healthy cholera into your belly" and "A cholera in your bones!" It must have been felt that bone cholera was more uncomfortable than the run-of-the-mill variety. Other ill-wishes included: "May he be thrown into an ague," "All problems I have in my heart should go to his head," "May you become famous — they should name a disease after you!" and "May your blood grow so healthy, your leeches' leeches need leeches!" Cholera was a distinct possibility in shtetl life, but anorexia nervosa was not a common ailment. A zaftig (plump) figure was a sign of affluence and a selling point for the local matchmaker, giving us the following curses: "May you never develop stomach trouble from too rich a diet." Definitely not a blessing but it sounds desirable next to "May you grow four stomachs like a cow, so that you get four times the bellyache and four times the heartburn."

Given the way in which shtetl life involved younger couples living with their parents, mother-in-law jokes were common, as one sees in this example from Jewish comedian Henny Youngman: "I just got back from a pleasure trip. I took my mother-in-law to the airport." In Yiddish culture, it was not only men who felt the wrath of a mother-in-law but women also. She could be constantly besieged by her mother-in-law in the home or the market. Here are two examples of women's disdain for mothers-in-law: "May your mother-in-law treat you like her own daughter and move in with you!" and "May your husband's father marry three times so that you have not one but three mothers-in-law!"

After having delighted in these creative examples of colourful Yiddish cursing, we will proceed in Part II to examine language that is "deranged" and realize that it can often be as gut-splittingly hilarious and witty as the arranged forms.

PART II

Deranged Wit

ℊ

"A word has its use, or like a man,
it will have a grave."
— Edwin Arlington Robinson

"How every fool can play upon the word."
— William Shakespeare, *The Merchant of Venice*

CHAPTER 1

ℬ

Malaprops

"A tax cut is really one of the anecdotes (antidotes)
to coming out of an economic illness."
— George W. Bush

ℬ NO PUN INTENDED?

The saying goes "A little knowledge is a dangerous thing." (Actually, the original line composed by Alexander Pope was "A little learning is a dangerous thing.") Sometimes, however, an inexact knowledge of words isn't so much perilous as just riotously hysterical.

There is a word in English to describe this type of mistake: malapropism, often shortened to malaprop. This term derives from Mrs. *Malaprop* (*mal à propos* — "inappropriate" in French), a character in Richard Brinsley Sheridan's 1775 play *The Rivals*, who has a penchant for this type of gaffe. She declares one man to be the "very *pineapple* of politeness," instead of *pinnacle*. She further states that a man is "as headstrong as an *allegory* (*alligator*) on the banks of the Nile."

Some of this character's other gaffes include "If I *reprehend* (*apprehend*) anything in this world, it is the use of my *oracular* (*vernacular*) tongue, and a nice *derangement* (*arrangement*) of *epitaphs* (*epithets*)!" and "Why killing's the matter! Why murder's the matter! But he can give you the *perpendiculars* (*particulars*)."

Although the term "malaprop" came into our language thanks to Sheridan's Mrs. Malaprop, other writers mined this concept well before Sheridan's era in the late eighteenth century. The Shakespearean character Dogberry in *Much Ado About Nothing* is particularly prone to them, and as a result the term "Dogberryism" exists as a synonym for malaprop. Here are some of his offerings:

> You are thought to be the most *senseless* (*sensible*) and fit man.

> Comparisons are *odorous* (*odious*).

> Thou shalt be condemned into everlasting *redemption* (*damnation* or *perdition*).

> Our watch, sir, have indeed *comprehended* (*apprehended*) two *auspicious* (*suspicious*) persons. . . .

Shakespeare wanted his audiences to laugh at Dogberry's misuse of language, but he also places the audience clearly in Dogberry's corner, when, at the end of the play, we are hoping that those in authority will have the sense to listen to Dogberry and be able to see through his malaprops as we have. Dogberry's use of language is the reverse of the establishment's; while everyone else in the play says things they don't mean, Dogberry means the things he doesn't say. Dogberry's great virtue is that his language never really gets in the way of his meaning.

So Sheridan's use of this seemingly accidental wordplay could have had a Shakespearian origin, but perhaps Sheridan was also inspired by Tobias Smollett's novel *The Expedition of Humphry Clinker*, which was published less than a decade earlier than *The Rivals*. In Smollett's epistolary novel, we read letters from two women, Tabitha Bramble and Winifred Jenkins, which feature many egregious malaprops. For example,

Winifred writes in one letter "the whole family has been in such *constipation* (*consternation*)" and in another, "O Mary Jones, pray without *seizing for grease* (*saving for grace*)." At her end of the correspondence, Tabitha writes, "I am astonished that Dr. Lewis should take upon him to give away Alderney, without my *privity* (*privacy*) and *concurrants* (*concordance*)," and in another rues that she leads "a life of an *indented* (*indentured*) slave." Many of her malaprops alert the reader to her preoccupation with sex, and Smollett's audience would undoubtedly not have missed the point of her repeated renderings of *accounts* as *accunts*.

It is perhaps telling, given the belief of eighteenth-century British males in their gender superiority, that the only two characters who mangle the English language in Smollett's novel are women. Was Smollett showing the inferiority of women through their inability to use language correctly? It is unclear, but particularly in the case of Tabitha, whose social position is higher than Winifred's, her myriad malaprops allow Smollett to make a statement regarding the many deficiencies of her personality.

Other more contemporary novelists have employed malaprops to paint a negative portrait of a character. For example, Mark Twain uses malaprops as a form of mocking humour in *The Adventures of Huckleberry Finn*. In one scene, Aunt Sally exclaims "I was *putrified* (*petrified*) with astonishment" and in another *Dauphin* is replaced by *Dolphin* and *funeral obsequies* degenerates into *funeral orgies*. Twain's use of malaprops by certain characters alerts the reader to the fact that the tales related by them may be somewhat fanciful.

Similarly, Barbara Kingsolver, in *The Poisonwood Bible*, creates the character Rachel, who accompanies her missionary father and three sisters to the Congolese jungle, as an utterly superficial and egocentric adolescent incapable of adjusting to her African environment. Kingsolver helps establish the negative aspects of her character when Rachel tells us (complete with malaprops): "Already I was heavy-hearted in my soul for the flush commode and machine-washed clothes and other simple things in life I have taken for *granite* (*granted*)." In another scene Rachel states, "My sisters gawked at the fascinating stranger and hung on his every *syllabus* (*syllable*) of English."

⚜ MODUS OPERANDI OF A MALAPROP

But how exactly does a malaprop come about? The Acoustical Society of America defines a malapropism as "a whole word that supplants an intended word," and adds that the words involved in malapropisms are related to each other in the way that they sound but not in their meanings. The humour in malaprops lies in the listener's awareness of the mistake and the speaker's ingenuousness. Thus, malaprops make us feel superior, for we wouldn't commit such a gaffe, would we?

Then again, maybe we would. It also helps if the replaced word lends a certain irony to the statement, like replacing *bonding* with *bondage*, *illegitimate* with *illiterate*, *erogenous* with *erroneous* or *monogamy* with *monotony*. It was in this ironic light that the magazine *New Scientist* related that an office worker described a colleague as "a vast *suppository* of information" rather than "a vast *repository* of information."

As a writer of language issues, particularly those giving rise to humour, I find that many of my acquaintances pass on amusing examples of howlers. Here are some of my favourites in the realm of malapropos:

> A friend related to me that his friend's father once came into a stuffy room and demanded, "Open da vinda Lionel, I'm *sophisticating (suffocating)*."

> Another friend mentioned to me recently that she grew up with someone prone to malaprops who once averred, "When a child gets to a certain age the *unbiblical (umbilical)* cord must be severed."

> At a union meeting that was punctuated by an individual unleashing a cacophony of obscenities, one acquaintance related that someone insisted, "Stop using so many *profundities (profanities)*."

> A former business associate told me that after he gave a eulogy at a family funeral, his cousin told him "that was the most touching *urology (eulogy)* I've ever heard."

At times, it is the particular context of a blooper that makes us howl. A friend who is a history professor at McGill University received a term paper from a student that dealt with relations between India and China. In it, the student wrote about the "*wonton* (*wanton*) aggression of the Chinese."

Over the years, I have written columns for several newspapers about malaprops where I asked readers to send me in some examples they had heard. Here are some of the responses:

My favorite malapropism involves my sister-in-law who upon returning from the ophthalmologist informed the collected company that she "has a *genital* (*genetic*) defect in her left eye."

Several years ago, my Jewish family's youngest daughter Wendy was commenting on a news item where some terrorists used gasoline bombs. In her own words, she said that they threw "*Mazel-tov* (*Molotov*) cocktails."

My late mother-in-law had a friend who went to the doctor for an *autopsy* (*biopsy*).

While travelling in Italy my wife was eating a plate of fried calamari when she said, "I like the calamari but I don't like the *testicles*" (*tentacles*).

My uncle told me about the depression his mother experienced following the birth of his brother: "She suffered from *post-mortem* (*post-partum*) depression."

A lady I knew told me that when her daughter was in labour, "the labour was taking so long that at one point the doctor had to go in and *seduce* (*induce*) her."

While chatting with a teacher acquaintance of mine, she excitedly told me that she was taking "an amazing *intercourse* course and learning so much." I wondered where I could take this course until I realized she meant she was taking it in *inter-session*.

Judge Robert Dnieper's courtroom in Toronto City Hall was always good for the occasional howler. A defendant having been found guilty was asked by the judge if he had anything to say prior to sentencing. His reply, "Well judge, there are *excruciating* (*extenuating*) circumstances in my case." Dnieper's reply: "They are about to become even more excruciating."

I know a woman who said that the doctor reported that her husband had died of a massive *internal fart* (*infarction*).

As can be seen from some of the doozies people sent me, medical mala-props are rampant, if not outright metastasizing. Recently, I chanced upon the mother of a long-time friend of mine, and I inquired as to the state of her husband's health. She informed me that her husband Nat's "*prostrate* (*prostate*) was acting up and that his *hemogoblin* (*hemoglobin*) was out-of-whack." I resisted a puerile temptation of inquiring as to her husband's acute *vagina* (*angina*) or to her *very close* (*varicose*) veins and *carnal* (*carpal*) tunnel syndrome.

Family physician David Spiegelman's book *Medical Malaprops* recounts some of the whoppers that he has heard from patients over a twenty-five-year span. They include:

I can't be pregnant because I had a tubal *litigation* (*ligation*).

My *utopian* (*fallopian*) tubes are blocked.

Another health professional who has garnered some juicy malapropos is Canadian Dr. Barry Wright who sent me a list of "some actual com-ments made by patients in my 41-year family practice of medicine." Included are:

Would you *exasperate* (*aspirate*) this cyst for me?

The eye doctor *diluted* (*dilated*) my pupils.

How's my systolic and *apostolic* (*diastolic*) blood pressure?

One also finds malaprops occasionally in the print and audio-visual media. These snafus should be caught by eagle-eyed editors but, alas, sometimes they are missed. I received this email in 2011 from a reader who saw an article I wrote about malaprops in the Canadian legal magazine *Lexpert*:

> Don Gillis, a highly-regarded dean of the New Brunswick legal community, died in 2005. The provincial newspaper [the *Telegraph-Journal*] ran a large front page article chronicling his distinguished career. The article included quotes from several of the leading members of the New Brunswick bar who commented on Gillis's accomplishments. One of the individuals quoted was Neil McKelvey, also a dean of the New Brunswick bar. The journalist who wrote the article, when mentioning McKelvey, interjected, "And the *platitudes* continued with Neil McKelvey. . . ."

Of course, the word he should have used was *plaudits*.

Even the somewhat erudite CBC is not above making these occasional slips. If you check the CBC podcast of *Out of Their Minds* from August 29, 2011, you will read this entry: "There's an old saying . . . even the mightiest oak starts out as a nut. . . . And when it comes to revolutionary change and paradigm-busting ideas and inventions, the people behind them start out as nuts. At least that's how they are perceived, fairly or unfairly. They are often ignored, ridiculed, and *ostersized* (*ostracized*)."

Similarly, the *Times Reporter* of Dover, Ohio, informed us in 1987 that "More of us will live to be *centurions*." Unless this story was dealing with some form of dystopia, I think the correct word should have been *centenarians*. Sometimes, even the headlines in newspapers produce malaprop howlers, as in 1978, when a headline in the Connecticut *Groton News* announced, "Police union to seek *blinding* (*binding*) arbitration."

While it can be fun when an uncle who might not have finished high school commits a malaprop, it is more enjoyable when some powerful person creates a gaffe, so I want to honour (or dishonour) some politicians who have mangled the glorious tongue of Shakespeare. One surname, however, stands far above the rest — Bush.

One reason given for the defeat of the Bush-Quayle ticket in 1992 was its inability to communicate with the electorate. Bush admitted that "fluency in English is something that I'm not accused of." During a speech, George Herbert Bush told a crowd of 15,000 in Ridgefield, New Jersey, how much he "appreciated their *recession* (*reception*)." This statement, however, had been topped by Dan Quayle in 1991 when he told a gathering that "Republicans understood the importance of *bondage* (*bonding*) between mother and child."

But "Poppa" couldn't hold a malapropian candle to his son Dubya. "Bushisms," aka "Bushspeak," aka "Bushonics" have been maligned by a host of literate commentators. For example, Stanford linguist Geoff Nunberg stated that "Bush's malaprops can make him sound like someone who learned the language over a bad cell phone connection." Here's a mere whiff of George W. Bush's snafus:

> My education message will *resignate* (*resonate*) among all parents.

> We cannot let terrorists and rogue nations hold this nation *hostile* (*hostage*).

> Keep good relations with the *Grecians* (*Greeks*).

> They *misunderestimated* (*misunderstood/underestimated*) me.

Also, Bush is supposed to have said to Tony Blair, "The problem with the French is that they don't have a word for entrepreneur." Alas, this was a well-conceived myth; too good to be true.

The Bushes are not the only Texans who have assaulted the English language with their malaprops. Former Speaker of the Texas House of Representatives Gibson Lewis is credited with this trinity: "I want to thank each of you for having *extinguished* (*distinguished*) yourselves this session; "I am filled with *humidity* (*humility*)"; and "this is *unparalysed* (*unparalleled*) in the state's history."

Political malaprops in the USA occasionally transcend Texans. Long-time Chicago mayor Richard J. Daley told a crowd: "We should strive for "greater *platitudes* (*plateaus*) of achievement." Sarah Palin, former Governor of Alaska, kept up the tradition of "grave new" Republican words in July 2010, when she tweeted, "Ground Zero Mosque supporters: doesn't it stab you in the heart, as it does ours throughout the heartland? Peaceful Muslims, pls *refudiate* (*repudiate/refute*)."

Palin's tweet was quickly deleted to be replaced with *refute*, but the clip of Palin's using the word, which was aired from July 2010 on Sean Hannity's Fox News program, remains with us. Commentators gave mixed reviews to Palin's coinage. William Kristol in the *Weekly Standard* stated, "We need a word that captures and conjoins the meaning of refutation and repudiation." What this right-wing commentator didn't add was his particular belief in the need for a word to refute and repudiate left-wing ideas. More typical was a reaction to Palin's neologism provided by satirist Andy Borowitz who said that if Palin ever became president, "her first official act will be to cancel the agreement between nouns and verbs."

This is not to say that American pols are the only ones decimating the English language. When former Australian Prime Minister Tony Abbott was opposition leader, he told the audience at a Liberal party event in Melbourne that "No one — however smart, however well-educated, however experienced — is the *suppository* (*repository*) of wisdom."

As a Canadian, I am aware that in "the true north, strong and free" politicians are also equally verbally inept. In fact, former Canadian Prime Minister Jean Chrétien was guilty of massacring both of Canada's official languages. Some years ago, Don Martin wrote in the *National Post* that "Chrétien can explode into an outstretched microphone without warning, his mangled syntax cascading forth as a rolling jumble of randomly sequenced verbs, nouns and adjectives which has left a generation of editors confounded." While Chrétien was often accused of committing malaprops, his gems were not technically such, but just unadulterated claptrap. An example of such was his assertion "A proof is a proof. What kind of a proof? It's a proof. A proof is a proof. And when you have a good proof, it's because it's proven."

This is not to say that in Canada only our highest political officials have unleashed some linguistic humdingers. John Kushner, a Calgary alderman during the 1960s, told a colleague, "don't get your *dandruff* (*dander*) up," and once stated, "I'm not sure very many of us can understand all this legal *jargle* (*jargon*)." Allan Lamport, mayor of Toronto from 1952 to 1954, is credited with saying, "I deny the allegation, and I deny the *allegators* (*those alleging*)." After retiring from politics he supposedly said, "I sold my house and moved into a *pandemonium* (*condominium*)." When backbencher Jack Horner was promoted to Trudeau's cabinet as a minister without portfolio in the 1970s, he was given a speech to read by one of his aides that included the word *panacea*. As Horner was not familiar with the word he rendered it as *pancreas*. For some time afterwards, civil servants would get a chuckle at meetings by saying with respect to proposals, "this is not a pancreas, you know."

My favourite Canadian political malaprop was committed by former British Columbian Socred Social Welfare Minister Phil Gaglardi in 1969. During a radio talk show, he said that his ministry might foot the bill for birth control pills for unwed mothers but only "when there were *extemporaneous* (*extenuating*) circumstances."

Perhaps, one shouldn't be too hard on offenders as it is the very artlessness of malaprops that makes them so endearing, or do I mean entertaining? And aside from the pure joy elicited from hearing someone mess up, malaprops are amusing because they sometimes reveal hidden connections between words. For this reason, it's interesting to see some of the errors that young children make, for one can often find that their mistaken words are quite logical. When I wrote my newspaper articles on malaprops, people occasionally shared some of the gems their kids came out with, such as calling an *icicle* an *ice tickle*, and an *umbrella* a *rainbrella*. *Kindergarten* became *kidney garter*, *kidneys* turned into *kid knees*, *Kleenex* into *clean nose* and a *gazebo* mutated into *gazebra*.

My own family and friends have also contributed to my stock of infantile malaprops. In February 2013, my daughter was listening to an NPR program when her four-year-old Judah was in the room. The host was discussing the *sequester* due to go into effect on March 1st that would affect billions in cuts to social programs. Judah wanted to know why the radio was discussing *Queen Esther*. (Queen Esther is the heroine in the

Biblical story of Purim, a tale Judah had just heard.) My partner Carol told me that when her daughter Beatrice was a little tot she referred to *flutterbys* instead of *butterflies*, and when she was unhappy told her mom that she was *upsad* (*sad* and *upset*).

One friend related to me that, while her daughter was away at summer camp, she wrote a letter complaining about her *dire rear* (*diarrhea*). Still another colleague reported that her precocious six-year-old son informed her that he was *black toast* (*lactose*) intolerant. In 2005, a reader shared with me that "my six-year old granddaughter came home from school and told her mom she needed $2 to help kids that were hit by the big *salami* (*tsunami*).

❧ HISTORY MALAPROPS

Perhaps because words fall into disuse over time, the field of history is a fertile breeding ground for malaprops. Here are some purportedly committed by students of the subject that I received in the last decade from readers, many of whom have been teachers. It seems that several of these bloopers appear in two books written by Richard Lederer, entitled *Anguished English* and *More Anguished English*. From these sources, here, in chronological order, is a malaproprian history of civilization:

> No human beings were found during the Ice Age because it was the *pre-stork* (*pre-historic*) era.

> The Great Wall of China was built to keep out the *Mongrels* (*Mongols*).

> The Ancient Greeks invented three kinds of columns: Corinthian, *ironic* (*ionic*), and *dorc* (*doric*) and built the *Apocalypse* (*Acropolis*).

> Homer wrote *The Iliad* and the *Oddity* (*Odyssey*).

> Socrates died from an overdose of *wedlock* (*hemlock*).

> Oedipus killed his father and married his real mother. That's called *incense* (*incest*).

The Romans prosecuted the early Christians because they disapproved of *gladiola* (*gladiator*) fights. . . .

The Jews were a proud people and throughout history they had trouble with unsympathetic *Genitals* (*Gentiles*).

The greatest writer of the *futile* (*feudal*) age was Chaucer.

In the Middle Ages many people died from the *bluebonnet* (*bubonic*) plague after growing *boobs* (*buboes*) on their necks.

Because people thought Joan of Arc was a witch they burned her at the *steak* (*stake*).

Henry VIII had a hard time walking because he had an *abbess* (*abscess*) on his knee.

Sir Francis Drake *circumcised* (*circumnavigated*) the world with a 100-foot clipper.

Queen Elizabeth's navy defeated the Spanish *armadillo* (*armada*).

William Shakespeare wrote tragedies, comedies . . . all in *Islamic* (*iambic*) pentameter.

Descartes' famous maxim was "cogito *eros* (*ergo*) sum."

Cyrus McCormick invented the McCormick *raper* (*reaper*), which did the job of 100 men.

Louis Pasteur discovered a cure for *rabbis* (*rabies*).

Thomas Edison was the inventor of . . . the *indecent* (*incandescent*) lamp.

In 1957, Eugene O'Neill won a *Pullet Surprise* (*Pulitzer Prize*).

J.S. Bach practised on an old *spinster* (*spinet*) in his attic.

J.S. Bach practised on an old spinster in his attic.

Not surprisingly, given the demise of religious education and practice, the domain of Bible studies also sports many malaprop heresies spouted by students:

> In the first book of the Bible, *Guinessis* (*Genesis*), God got tired of creating the world so he took the Sabbath off.

> Jacob had a brother named *Seesaw* (*Esau*).

> The seventh commandment is thou shalt not *admit* (*commit*) adultery.

> King David defeated the *Finkelsteins* (*Philistines*).

> Solomon, one of David's sons, had 300 wives and 700
> *porcupines* (*concubines*).

> When Mary heard she was the mother of Jesus, she sang the
> *Magna Carta* (*Magnificat*).

> Jesus was born because Mary had an immaculate
> *contraception* (*conception*).

> The epistles were the wives of the *apostals* (*apostles*).

> St. Paul *cavorted* (*converted*) to Christianity; he preached holy
> *acrimony* (*matrimony*), which is another name for marriage.

> It's the *scatological* (*eschatological*) perspective of Christians
> that gives us Hope. . . .

Is it those students who are not well-travelled who easily mangle geographic references? The following place names take a beating, ending up as malaprops:

> The Israelites lived in the *Sarah* (*Sahara*) Desert and
> travelled by *Camelot* (*camel, a lot*).

> Moses went up Mount *Cyanide* (*Sinai*) for the Ten
> Commandments but died before he reached *Canada*
> (*Canaan*).

> Pompeii was destroyed by an overflow of *saliva* (*lava*).

> The capital of Ethiopia is *Adidas* (*Addis*) Ababa.

❧ POP CULTURE MALAPROPS

We also see many deliberate malaprops in popular culture that make us chuckle. The program *All in the Family* had some memorable ones. In it, the central character Archie Bunker told his wife Edith that if she was experiencing *minstrel* (*menstrual*) pains while *administrating* (*menstruating*) she should see the *groinecologist* (*gynecologist*). He also railed against the *vagrant* (*flagrant*) disregard for the law by the youth of today. While *consecrating* (*concentrating*) on the evening newspaper he informed his "meathead" son-in-law that the Pope was *inflammable* (*infallible*). Jewish men, he claimed, wore *yamahas* (*yarmulkes*) on their heads.

The writers for the program *The Sopranos* kept up this malapropian tradition and I suspect, given the pervasive graphic violence of the series, the bloopers were often added to supply some comic relief. Here were some of my favourites:

> There's no *stigmata* (*stigma*) with going to a shrink.

> Let's create a little *dysentery* (*dissent*) in the ranks.

> I was *prostate* (*prostrate*) with grief.

> She's an *albacore* (*albatross*) around my neck.

> He could technically not have *penisary* (*penile*) contact with her *Volvo* (*vulva*).

> We're in a f****** *stagmire* (*quagmire*).

During a meal, Paulie, one of Tony Soprano's henchmen, is warbling on about his theory of what caused the extinction of the dinosaurs. A woman then asks, "Wasn't that a *meteor*?" Paulie's rejoinder: "They're all *meat-eaters*."

Saturday Night Live, that end-of-the-week joy fest, has also bequeathed us some malaprop TV pearls. For example, Gilda Radner played a character, Emily Litella, who wondered why people worried about "*violins* (*violence*) on television, *jewelry* (*Jewry*) in the Soviet Union and endangered *feces* (*species*)." Also, she didn't understand why people were so concerned about *peanuts in Regina* (*penis in vagina*) and was bemused by all the talk she heard about a presidential *erection* (*election*). She also spoke out against the practice of *busting* (*bussing*) schoolchildren for the purpose of integration. When her faux pas were exposed, her weak rejoinder was "never mind."

Given my Jewish roots, it seems fitting to end with a malapropian joke told to me some years ago by a rabbi. It goes like this:

Rivkah went to her doctor for a check-up. Afterwards, the doctor said to her, "I must inform you that you have a *fissure* in your uterus, and if you ever have a baby it would be a *miracle*." As soon as she got home, Rivkah said to her husband, "You vouldn't belief it. I vent to the doctah and he told me" — "You haf a *fish* in your uterus and if you haf a baby it vill be a *mackerel*."

So far with malaprops, we have looked at derangements that occur unconsciously in the brain, and which can be replicated as wordplay to create humour. In the next chapter, we can locate the precise anatomical position where the derangement most often occurs — it's in the ears.

CHAPTER 2

g

Mondegreens

"I want a girl just like the girl that
harried dear old dad."

g HEARING IS IN THE EAR OF THE BEHOLDER

Growing up in the drug-hazed '60s, I pondered the identity of the enigmatic Leslie referenced in the popular song "Groovin" by the Rascals:
"You and me and Leslie." Leslie, however, was a figment of my imagination, or more precisely of my imagined hearing. The lyric, I found out
years later, was "You and me endlessly." I had been "mondegreened."

The term "mondegreen" was coined by writer Sylvia Wright. As a child
she had heard the Scottish ballad "The Bonny Earl of Murray" which
she interpreted thus:

> Ye Highlands and ye lowlands
> Oh where have you been?

> They hae slay the Earl of Murray
> And Lady Mondegreen.

Sylvia Wright was wrong in believing that two murders had been committed. The "Lady Mondegreen" was a projection of her romantic imagination, for the last line in fact was not "Lady Mondegreen" but *laid him on the green*.

Children are particularly prone to this type of mistake, where an unfamiliar word or phrase heard is changed into something more familiar. This process has created some memorable "religious" personages such as "Round John Virgin" (round yon Virgin), "Harold be thy name" (hallowed be thy name) and "Gladly, the cross-eyed bear" (gladly, the cross I'd bear). Although "Olive" is strictly not a religious character, I'd be remiss if I didn't provide honourable mention here to the yuletide character, who appears to the aurally-challenged as "Olive, the other reindeer," in the lyric "All of the other reindeer. . . ."

O Canada, we stand on cars and freeze.

The majority of mondegreens occur in the lyrics of songs. Years ago, word maven William Safire cited an American grandmother who interpreted the line "A girl with kaleidoscope eyes" in the Beatles' song "Lucy in the Sky with Diamonds" as "A girl with colitis goes by." The lyric "'scuse me while I kiss the sky" from Jimi Hendrix's song "Purple Haze" was interpreted by some fans as "'scuse me while I kiss this guy." Hendrix was aware of this misinterpretation and sometimes during a performance he would help perpetuate the misunderstanding by kissing a male band member after singing the line.

A friend related to me that for years he couldn't understand why singer Robert Palmer was dissing Michael Jackson in his song "Addicted to Love." Then, one day he had an aural epiphany and realized that the lyric he supposed was "a dick with a glove," was, in fact, "addicted to love."

Truth be known, there are some song lyrics that are almost impossible to decipher. One such is The Pretenders' song "Brass in Pocket (I'm special)," with the lyric "Gone is my _____." I had several candidates for this blanked word, such as "senses," "saucy," "sassy," "sausage," and "sashay," but I wasn't remotely close, as the word I couldn't decipher turned out to be "side-step." I suspect few people know that the lyric that follows "Willie and the poor boys are playin'" in Credence Clearwater Revival's song "Down on the Corner" is "bring a nickel tap your feet." Still it's a wonder that someone at the website kissthisguy.com, which is dedicated to misheard lyrics, reported hearing this lyric as "singing pickles can't be beat." Also by this musical group is the misinterpreted lyric "There's a bad moon on the rise" which has been known to be heard as "There's a bathroom on the right." Naturally, uncommon words are more likely to be misheard. Maria Muldaur's song entitled "Midnight at the Oasis" has been interpreted as "Midnight after you're wasted."

On the aforementioned website dedicated to misheard lyrics, kissthisguy.com, I noticed that in Sarah McLachlan's "Building a Mystery," her lyric "you strut your rasta wear and your suicide poem" was interpreted as "you stretched your ass to where in a suicide home." In the Aerosmith song "Dude Looks like a Lady," the titled lyric is somewhat squealed, resulting in my always having thought the line was "Do the funky lady."

This website confirmed that I was not the only befuddled listener; others had variously misheard this line as "Do the shockalayley," "Do the rock-a lady" and "Doodoos like a lady."

Some mishearings are particularly incredible given the clarity and renown of the lyrics. Bob Dylan's line "The answer my friend is blowin' in the wind" has apparently been interpreted entomologically as "The ants are my friends. . . ." At kissthisguy.com somebody claims to have heard the lyric "No dark sarcasm in the classroom" from Pink Floyd's "Another Brick in the Wall" as "No Dukes of Hazzard in the classroom."

Of course, as in other domains of wit, in some cases the lyrics of songs have been deliberately revised for irreverent purposes. Here are some cases in point:

Here comes the bride. All fat and wide.

Jimmy crapped corn and I don't care.

And more recently, the Beatles lyric, "She was a day tripper. . . ." morphed into "She was a gay stripper. . . ."

I'd like to give the last word on mondegreens to cognitive scientist Steven Pinker. In his book *The Language Instinct* he says that the "interesting thing about mondegreens is that the mis-hearings are generally less plausible than the intended lyrics." He relates the anecdote of a student who heard a line from the Shocking Blue song "I'm Your Venus" as "I'm your penis. I'm your fire at your desire." The student was amazed it wasn't censored.

So far, we have investigated several suspects in the alleged crime of aiding and abetting the derangement process. We have castigated twits, half-wits, politicians and celebrities to name but a few. Even parts of your upper torso, such as the brain and the ears have been profiled for scrutiny. In the next chapter we will cast our aspersions on another candidate responsible for the "derangement" process — the English language itself.

ℊ

Mangled English

"Sometimes you have to believe that all English
speakers should be committed to an asylum for the verbally
insane. In what other language do people drive in a
parkway and park in a driveway? In what other language
do people recite at a play and play at a recital?"
— Richard Lederer

ℊ HOW THE LANGUAGE OF THE
ANGLO-SAXONS CAN BE MANGLED

As we have seen, it is easy to make mistakes in English when it is your
first language, so you can picture the high probability of committing
errors when it's a second language, and you don't understand the idiomatic structure of English. Idioms are the anomalies of language, the rebels
of the linguistic world. They are what give a language much of its colour,
but they can be rather frustrating to someone who is trying to learn or
translate a language in a logical fashion, because often idioms aren't
logical at all. The word "idiom" comes from the Greek *idios* which means
"own, private, peculiar," and in case you're wondering, the word "idiot"

also comes from the same Greek source. This peculiarity of idioms leads to a breaking of rules in two ways: semantically by their meanings, and syntactically by their grammar.

The problem with the words found in idioms is that they don't mean what you think they're going to mean. For example, a "bucket" means a "pail" and to "kick" means to "strike with the foot." But, of course, to *kick the bucket* does not mean to move the pail with your foot; it means "to die." The meaning of the whole is not the sum of the meanings of the parts. Also, the context determines if we're dealing with an idiomatic expression or not. If I spill the beans on the table it's not idiomatic, I just have a messy table. But if I idiomatically *spill the beans* — it is clear to someone whose first language is English that I am revealing a secret.

When working at a predominantly French-speaking corporation, I had occasion to experience the confusion of unfamiliar expressions such as *peter le feu* which taken literally means "to fart fire." I pondered what sort of odoriferous establishment I worked in until someone assuaged my consternation by informing me that the idiom meant "enthusiastic." I didn't even want to think what the expression *se peter les bretelles* meant until I checked a dictionary that translated this idiom literally as "to break one's suspenders," and the expression actually means "to boast." I was also bewildered by *j'aime pas sa fraise*. Why would anybody object to someone's strawberry, or to any fruit one possesses? I was ultimately enlightened by a co-worker that here the expression *fraise* referred to "face."

I remember one incident that particularly accentuated the difficulty of idioms for the second-language English speaker and, although I spoke more French than English to my fellow employees, with some of my French-speaking friends we would alternate evenly between Canada's two official languages. The incident occurred when I was about to leave for a well-deserved summer vacation. Well-deserved because my workload had been particularly hectic and stressful for several months. One of my work colleagues named Serge told me in English, "Howard, you look really tired, why don't you *rest in peace* on your vacation?" Of course, what Serge was advising was logical. I definitely needed both "rest" and "peace," but when I told him the meaning of *rest in peace* in English we both had a good laugh.

ℵ ANGUISHED IDIOMATIC ENGLISH TRANSLATIONS

We have seen that we can't assume communication is being effected, even when native speakers of English are conversing. Not surprisingly then, this "Manglish" increases dramatically when English is being translated from another language. Many translators tell me this is particularly so when dealing with idiomatic English, and they often go as far as to consider idioms their *bête noire*.

Never assume that an expression means the same in English as it does in another language. Take the English expression *in the wind*, meaning something is "under way." In French, the equivalent expression *dans l'air* at one time referred to someone who is "with it." Italians who are "with it" are said "to have their hands in the dough," whereas in French this idiom means "pitching in." However, Spaniards with "hands in the dough" aren't "with it" or "pitching in" at all; they've been caught "red-handed." Pity the poor translator!

Languages vary quite a bit not only in their expressions and vocabulary but also in their use of pronouns, and this too can lead to translations that bring a smile. My son-in-law Noah was amused some years ago while cooking meat at an Israeli kibbutz when an Israeli girl whose mother tongue was Hebrew told him, "You have to burn her, she's still alive" instead of "You have to cook it, it's still raw."

Sometimes translations neglect the context and are so bad that they are hilarious. The following was passed on to me by an employee who worked at the Berlitz office in Montreal: *"Pénétrez dans la voiture, restez en érection dans le siège et passez le ceinture au travers des cuisses."* You might guess that a sex manual was the source of the above, but in fact, before being poorly translated into French, it was this rather tame phrase from a car manual: "Enter the car, sit erect in the seat and pull the belt across your lap."

What can sometimes be lost in translating menus from English to French is the desire for the food and beverage. A finger sandwich loses its appeal when it is transformed into *"sandwich de doigts"* (literally, a sandwich of fingers), as do cocktail mixers when they are mutated from *"diluants"* (most common literal translation is "paint thinners"). A restaurant featuring "Virgin olive oil chicken breast sandwich" had this item transmogrified into French as an affront to chastity: *"sandwich de la vièrge à la poitrine de poulet."*

✤ POOR TRANSLATIONS IN THE POLITICAL ARENA

Not surprisingly, some less-than-stellar translations have led to diplomatic incidents or awkward moments. For example, former Soviet leader Nikita Khrushchev was told during a television interview in the USA that he was "barking up the wrong tree": literally, that he was wrong. Russians were outraged when this idiomatic expression was interpreted as their leader "baying like a hound." As if to revenge the Warsaw Bloc, then American President Jimmy Carter, on a tour of Poland, wanted to communicate, "I have a strong desire to know the Polish people." Through the ineptness of a translator, that "knowledge" came out stronger and more biblically than Carter intended. The message that emerged was "I desire the Polish people carnally." This same translator sowed potential seeds of defection with Carter's "When I left the U.S. . . ." rendered as "When I abandoned the U.S. . . ."

Some years ago when then British Prime Minister Tony Blair was addressing the Canadian Parliament, he related one of his translation faux pas. Blair had invited the French prime minister at the time, Lionel Jospin, to participate in a joint press conference in French and English on live television. Relatively bilingual, Blair was asked in French whether he was jealous of Jospin's success. He meant to say that he was envious of Jospin's magnificent positions taken on different issues, instead of which he startled the French public by saying that he desired Jospin in many different positions. *"J'ai toujours envie de Lionel de toutes les facons."*

Faux amis (false friends) words that have come into English from French but not with the same sense, are ripe for mangling the language. Known to have caused diplomatic stirs at the United Nations, *faux amis* were to blame when the USA State Department took affront at a note from the French government that began, *Nous demandons*, because it was ineptly translated literally as a demand rather than a request. Once again at the United Nations, a passage that described the collapse of Western Europe as "brutal" created much international tension until it was realized that it had been translated literally from French where, in this context, the sense of brutal corresponds more to the English "serious" than "savage."

A 1905 draft of a treaty between Russia and Japan was written in English and French opening up the opportunity for *faux amis* style *faux pas*. The document treated the English "control" and the French *contrôler* as equivalent, notwithstanding the fact that in English the word connotes dominance, while in French it simply means "to inspect." As a result of this misinterpretation, the treaty came close to collapsing.

These misinterpretations, however, seem trivial compared to one that may have contributed to the death of over 130,000 people. At the Potsdam Declaration on July 26, 1945, Japan was ordered to surrender unconditionally. In response, the Japanese Cabinet stated that Japan was giving the peace offer *mokusatsu*, which can mean either "we are considering it," or "we are ignoring it." The Domei news agency in Japan rendered the word in English to mean "ignore," when the sense may well have been "consider." Partly as a result of this misinterpretation, on August 6, 1945, Harry Truman ordered an atomic bomb, which killed over 90,000 people, to be dropped on Hiroshima. On August 9th, over 40,000 Japanese died when a second atomic bomb was dropped on Nagasaki.

Little wonder Italians claim *traduttore-traditore*, "a translator is a traitor." The poor translator, albeit unwittingly, could also become a killer, as in the Japanese example.

❧ ADVERTISING SLOGANS

Not surprisingly, the difficulty in translating properly has led to some advertising snafus. Advertising slogans attempt to enhance a consumer's desire for a product being promoted. When the slogan is translated into another language, the product's appeal is often lost in translation. In some cases, the appeal is turned into downright embarrassment. Chicken magnate Frank Perdue's line, "It takes a tough man to make a tender chicken," is bound to make the chaste chicken lover (not to mention the chaste chicken) blanch when translated into Spanish: "It takes a sexually stimulated man to make a chicken affectionate." When Parker Pen marketed a ballpoint pen in Mexico, its ads were supposed to have read, "It won't leak in your pocket and embarrass you." Instead, the company thought that the word *embarazar*, "to impregnate," meant "to embarrass" — a classic *faux amis* — so the ad read: "It won't leak in your pocket and make you pregnant."

Even a wholesome product like milk can curdle when translated into Spanish. The American Dairy Association's huge success with its "Got milk?" campaign landed them in trouble when they tried to expand the promotion to Mexico. The Spanish translation they used conveyed the following: "Are you lactating?"

Of course, it isn't only the Spanish language that lends itself to changing the intent of English commercial messages, nor is this process particularly new. When Ford first sold Model Ts in Russia, its brochure recommended washing the car with "Ivory Soap." But when translated into Russian the instructions advised using soap made from elephant tusks. Pepsi's famed slogan, "Come alive with the Pepsi generation," when translated by a Chinese-language newspaper in Taiwan, emerged as the uninviting "Pepsi helps bring your ancestors back from the grave." Surprisingly, the German translators handled the Pepsi slogan similarly to the Chinese. It emerged as "Come out of the grave with Pepsi." These may be apocryphal tales, but there is probably some basis in fact, and one can see how the idiomatic nature of English could be misinterpreted by ad execs.

Other commercial translations into German haven't fared any better than those of Pepsi. The hair products company, Clairol, introduced the "Mist Stick," a curling iron, into Germany only to find out that "mist" is a slang word for "manure." Needless to say, it wasn't a big seller, especially for brunettes. When Vicks first introduced its cough drops into the German market, they were chagrined to learn that the German pronunciation of *V* is *F*, thus rendering the term as the guttural equivalent of "carnal acts." The firm ended up re-naming the product Wick for the German market. Not to be outdone, the tissue company Puffs tried to introduce its product to the Germans, only to learn that "puff" in German is a colloquial term for a whorehouse. Unfortunately, the product wasn't a big hit in England either, as "puff" can designate a homosexual or an emasculated man.

A loss in translation can also occur when a foreign-based product is marketed in English-speaking countries. In Scandinavian languages, the word for vacuum cleaner derives from its function of sucking up dust. Swedish-based Electrolux decided that its United Kingdom slogan should convey the powerful swooshing quality of its product. The Swedish "Nothing vacuums like Electrolux" emerged in English as a slogan with rhyme but no reason: "Nothing sucks like Electrolux."

One might even have the actual translation of a campaign down to the last detail, but cultural knowledge of the country concerned can still remain imperative. When Colgate introduced a toothpaste in France called "Cue," either no one within the company knew, or wanted to admit that they knew, that "Cue" is the name of an infamous French pornography magazine. One can imagine a pen manufacturer marketing their product in France as "le pen" and finding out that a larger portion of the population are boycotting it because of it bearing the same name as extremist right-wing politician Jean-Marie Le Pen, or his daughter Marine Le Pen.

℘ WORLD ENGLISH SIGNS

With English becoming the international language, people have espied some peculiar English signs in the global village. Although examples are rampant on the Internet, I first became acquainted with many of the following when reading Richard Lederer's *Anguished English*. Others have been sent to me by eagle-eyed friends who have visited some exotic locales:

> In a Bucharest hotel lobby: The lift is being fixed for the next day. During that time we regret that you will be unbearable.

> In a Yugoslav hotel: The flattening of underwear with pleasure is the job of the chambermaid.

> In a Japanese hotel: You are invited to take advantage of the chambermaid.

> In the lobby of a Moscow hotel across from a Russian monastery: You are welcome to visit the cemetery where

famous Russian and Soviet composers, artists, and writers are buried daily except Thursday.

On the menu of a Swiss restaurant: Our wines leave you nothing to hope for.

Alongside a Hong Kong tailor's shop: Ladies may have a fit upstairs.

At a French Riviera hotel: Swimming is forbidden in the absence of a savior.

Customers who find our waitresses rude ought to see our managers.

Advertisement for donkey rides in Thailand: Would you like to ride on your own ass?

At a Prague tourist agency: Take one of our horse-driven city tours. We guarantee no miscarriages.

In a Nairobi restaurant: Customers who find our waitresses rude ought to see our managers.

In a Zurich hotel: Because of the impropriety of entertaining guests of the opposite sex in the bedroom, it is suggested that the lobby be used for this purpose.

In a Norwegian cocktail lounge: Ladies are requested not to have children in the bar.

Beijing road sign: Execution in progress.

In a Tokyo bar: Special cocktails for the ladies with nuts.

Unintentional mutilation of the English language by those for whom it isn't their mother tongue is almost excusable compared with the derangement process covered in the following chapter. This form of linguistic bruising can be summed up succinctly by an embarrassing four-letter word — oops!

CHAPTER 4

⅋

Typos & Editorial Bloopers

"Errare humanum est"
(to err is human)
— Seneca the Younger

⅋ AN EMBARASMENT OF MISPRINTS

Beware, writers! Your perceived sexual proclivity can be contingent on the omission of a vowel. Alas, I speak from personal experience. Some years ago, I emailed a friend's daughter who lives in Mexico to get details of a vacation hideaway that she had visited, called Pie de la Cuesta. I meant to write that I would be travelling with my partner "Carol," but I left out one of the two vowels in her name. So when my friend was speaking to her daughter a couple of days later, the daughter dumbfounded her mother by saying, "I didn't know Howard was gay?" Her mother informed her that she was fairly certain that my tendencies were firmly in the heterosexual camp to which the daughter responded, "He definitely is gay. He said he's coming to Mexico with his partner Carl."

Missing letters can be even more embarrassing: take the case of the word "public." Opera singer Beverly Sills' 1976 autobiography entitled *Bubbles: A Self-Portrait* began with a seemingly too-revealing opening sentence: "When I was only three, and still named Belle Miriam Silverman, I sang my first aria in *pubic*." The publishers, aghast, rounded up all the copies they could locate and issued a second *public* "first edition." Deletion of an "l" in the word has also led to groups such as "The Pubic Record Office" and the official to be named "Director of Pubic Prosecutions." This same typo was committed by the *Senior Times* of Montreal some years ago. A story dealt with a building that wanted its residents to feel safe, and the paper reported that it had installed "infrared lights in all *pubic* places."

Village Voice some years ago reviewed Mary Chase's 1945 play *Harvey* and provided an ecclesiastic allusion when an animal was intended. It declared that the play's protagonist was accompanied everywhere by "an invisible six-foot-tall white *rabbi*," proving that even letters can be circumcised.

Perhaps the most famous typo of all time occurred in 1631 when Robert Barker and Martin Lucas, both royal printers in London, published what was supposed to be a word-for-word reprint of the 1611 King James Bible. Unfortunately, they omitted a whole word, thereby rendering the seventh commandment as *Thou shalt commit adultery*. Not surprisingly, this holy book came to be known as "The Wicked Bible." The British Parliament was not amused and ordained that all copies of this edition of the Bible be destroyed. It also fined the London publisher £300 for this heretical, yet hedonistic, omission. Eighty-three years after its printing, Joseph Addison commented on this edition in *The Spectator*: "By the Practice of the World, which prevails in this degenerate Age, I am afraid that very many young Profligates, of both Sexes, are possessed of this spurious Edition of the Bible, and observe the Commandment according to that faulty Reading." Lighten up, Joseph.

Deletion of text was a common occurrence in pre-cyber days. Type then consisted of metal objects that were carried around and sometimes "miscarried." In 1960, the *New York Times* did a story on Yvonne de Gaulle, the wife of Charles de Gaulle, when the couple was in New

York. The *Times* stated that Madame de Gaulle "tries to avoid charitable works." What the *Times* intended saying was that Madame de Gaulle "tries to avoid *publicity but is active* in charitable works." Presumably type was misplaced and the headline was "de-ranged." Alas, history informs us that it is not unknown for French leaders to suffer savage "cuts."

As witnessed by the omission of "not" from the aforementioned "Wicked Bible," a deletion need not be as large as the presumed miscarriage of type in the de Gaulle de-rangement to be devastating. On October 3, 1980, *The Evening Times* of West Palm Beach, Florida, forgot the prefix *un-* before a word, and reported, very politically incorrectly, that "Despite our best efforts, black *employment* is still rising."

Now, all *Star Trek* fans know that space is the last frontier, but it can also be the lost frontier. Decades ago, *The New Haven Connecticut Register* featured a story about a governor who had a plethora of bills to enact at the close of a legislative session. In order to communicate this, the headline was supposed to read: "Governor's Pen is Busy Over Weekend." Unfortunately, the Governor's utensil of choice was altered when the headline was inadvertently rendered without spacing between the words to read: "Governor'sPenisBusyOverWeekend."

Forgetting spaces between words is by no means the only error with headlines. They can be de-ranged in a variety of ways. In the 1940s, American President Franklin Roosevelt was laid up in bed with a cold. Because of a typo, the headline in the *Washington Post* suggested that Roosevelt was laid up with something more enticing than a cold: "FDR in Bed with Coed." Roosevelt reportedly convulsed in laughter when he saw the headline (I'm sure Eleanor did not), then phoned the newspaper and ordered a hundred copies to be sent to his friends. Sadly, this presidential order was not enacted, because the circulation department had scurried about retrieving and shredding the incriminating remaining copies of the edition.

Typos involving politicians are not, however, always due to the mistakes of newspapers. On October 14, 2010, the *Chicago Sun-Times* reported that the name of Green Party gubernatorial candidate Rich Whitney was misspelled "Rich Whitey" on electronic-voting machines in twenty-three wards, about half of them in predominantly African-

American areas. The story added that officials said the error could not be corrected before Election Day. (As Whitney only had 2 per cent of the vote at the time of the typo, it is unlikely that it was responsible for his subsequent defeat.)

This typo involving ethnicity pales in comparison to one committed in 2010 by Penguin Australia. A recipe in *The Pasta Bible* called for "freshly ground black pepper" but, unfortunately, the last word in the recipe was rendered as "people." The publisher had to pulp 7,000 copies of the book. As one would expect in today's "no publicity is bad publicity" world, however, sales of the cookbook increased dramatically after the public became aware of the gaffe. Maybe not so de-ranged language, after all?

Nor do animal lovers escape the unpleasant effects of typos. In 1962, the *New York Times* printed a dinner menu that it then rated in its "reasonably priced" category. They offended dog owners, however, when the first course was listed as "consommé with poodles" instead of "consommé with noodles."

One pair of words prone to confusion/misprint is the tandem of navel/naval. In 1993, the *Manchester Cricket* (MA) said that the author of a new maritime book "is known as the master of the navel confrontation novel." Similarly, in June 21, 1999, *Time* magazine's Janice M. Horowitz advised "if you have congenital heart disease and can't resist a naval ring, be sure to ask for preventive antibiotics." Perhaps the Navy was not amused.

Some other snafus that have occurred in the media include the following:

> US Banks Wrestle with Argentine Deb. — *Duluth News-Tribune*

> Author Leo Rosten began an article with the words "As therapists are well aware . . ." and claims it emerged in print as "As the rapists are well aware . . ." — *Look* magazine

> In Chicago five men were accused of bride taking. — *Chicago News*

In the early 1970s, Princess Anne was a competitive horse show jumper. One headline praising her early lead in an event inadvertently lauded her

In Chicago, five men were accused of bride taking.

baking skills or, worse still, some other talents the Royals did not want advertised. The headline stated: "Princess Anne made an impressive tart" (*Birmingham Evening Mail*). The first pressing of Duane Eddy's 1962 version of *Londonderry Air* (flip side of *The Avenger*) was rendered as *London Derriere*. A British folkloric typo involves the dedication and subsequent traversing of a bridge in Manchester by Queen Victoria. It is claimed that a headline in the London *Times* supposedly reported, "Her Majesty cut the ribbon and pissed over the bridge." Methinks this pithy tale is apocryphal.

⅊ DERANGED HEADLINES
Now in the twenty-first century, websites such as fun-with-words.com and cheezburger.com are littered with supposed headlines such as "Include Your Children When Baking Cookies," and "Ike Says Nixon Can't Stand Pat" (his wife's name was Pat). More than an error with a letter or two, with spacing or with the odd word, headlines appearing in

print without their combination of words being checked for meaning result in very amusing derangements. Since these headlines are not documented, we will assume that they are apocryphal. Occasionally though, the source of the headline is cited and, strangely, several of these attributable headlines have a Bill Clinton connection. We have: "Women Lay Observers At Council" (*The Times*) and "Starr Aghast At First Lady Sex Position" (The *Washington Times*). I must admit to being particularly skeptical about the veracity of the headline "Clinton Stiff On Withdrawal" as it's just too apropos to be true, as well as being attributed to a newspaper with the rather suspicious name of *The Bosnia Bugle*.

Several of these headline howlers are, however, documented in a book entitled *Red Tape Holds Up New Bridge* whose content is a series of flubs collected by the *Columbia Journalism Review* in 1987. The title, with its unfortunate suggestion that substandard materials have been used in the construction of a bridge, derives from a headline that appeared in the *Milford Citizen* on July 12, 1982.

Some other confusing and diverting headlines include the following:

Retired priest may marry Springsteen — *Bloomington Indiana Herald-Times* 5/12/85

Never Withhold Herpes Infection From Loved One — *Albuquerque Journal* 12/26/84

Chef throws his heart into helping feed needy — *Louisville Courier-Journal* 11/22/85

Flier to duplicate Miss Earhart's fatal flight — *New Jersey Herald* 1/9/84

Most newspapers delight in sporting colourful headline stories. At the *Montreal Gazette* in the 1970s, there was a story about a portrait of then Canadian Prime Minister Pierre Trudeau. The headline declared "You Too Can Be Hung Like Trudeau." Even diacritical marks in headlines can be problematic. Some years ago, the same *Gazette* wanted to convey multicultural New Year's greetings in its headline using many languages, one of them being Spanish. "Happy New Year" in Spanish is *Feliz Año*

Nuevo, but since the *Gazette* had a style policy of rendering only accents in French, it printed the message as *Feliz Ano Nuevo*. This elicited torrents of Spanish protests because by eschewing the correct diacritical mark, the newspaper's glaring headline had wished people a "Happy New Asshole."

Having covered most of the types of English language mishmashes that lead to humorous results, I've reserved my personal bugbear for last. In the concluding chapter we will look at the rampant phenomenon that "deranges" me: the pleonasm.

CHAPTER 5

ᵹ

Pleonasm

"When large numbers of men are unable to
find work, unemployment results."
— Calvin Coolidge, President of USA, 1923–1929

ᵹ WE ARE TOTALLY SURROUNDED (ON ALL SIDES)
   BY REDUNDANCIES

Mercifully, it takes but a single word to describe verbal redundancy. The
term is "pleonasm," defined by the *OED* as "the use of more words in a
sentence than are necessary to express the meaning." It derived from the
Latin *pleonasmus* which, in turn, came from the Greek *pleonasmos* (more-
ness). Antony's line in *Julius Caesar*, "the *most* unkind*est* cut of all," is an
example of a pleonasm done for effect. Similarly, God says to Moses in
Exodus 3:14, "I am that I am." After what happened to Lot's wife in
Genesis 19, Moses was probably squeamish about accusing the Burning
Bush of redundancy. So, while oxymoron (Part I, Chapter 5) juxtaposes
opposites, pleonasm repeats itself for no discernible reason.

I first became aware of this penchant for verbal diarrhea back in 1993. CBC journalist Hana Gartner was interviewing then Prime Minister of Canada Jean Chrétien, who asserted that he was respected by most Quebecers, and that it was only the intellectual intelligentsia who disparaged him. Chrétien was following in the flowing tradition exemplified by fellow North American politicians. The man who provided impeachment insurance for George Herbert Bush, former Vice President Dan Quayle, said in a 1988 speech, "I got through a number of things in the area of defense, like showing the importance of cruise missiles and getting them more accurate so that we can have precise precision," and later in 1989 stated, "If we don't succeed, we run the risk of failure." Lest it seem that politicians in the USA are more prone to redundancy, in 2012, Mr. Chrétien was joined in his verbal overkill by Canadian Brian Pallister, leader of the Progressive Conservative party in Manitoba, who expressed his hope that "Everyone will enjoy themselves this holiday season, even you infidel atheists."

One does not have to be a North American politician to be redundant, however. Billy Snedden, the leader of the Liberal Party in Australia, declared in 1974, "We didn't lose the election because they got more votes than we did. We just got less than them."

Occasionally, even a non-politician is capable of these epiphanies. Actress Brooke Shields once declared, "Smoking can kill you, and if you've been killed, you've lost a very important part of your life," and former football coach Tom Landry averred, "Football is an incredible game. Sometimes it's so incredible, it's unbelievable."

These are some of the more egregious examples of redundant language but yea, we are not drowning in a bog of unnecessary words but in a veritable swampland. Why can't things be merely null, why do they have to be void as well? If I look in every nook, must I explore every cranny? Must I desist when I cease, abet when I aid, choose when I pick, and rave when I rant? Can't I just cease, aid, pick and rant? When we talk about "complete annihilation," "false pretenses," "foreign imports," "frozen tundra," "burning embers," "close proximity," an "uphill climb," a couple being "joined together," a "lesbian woman," and a woman "pregnant with child," I ponder, what are the alternatives?

Have you ever seen a young geezer, a non-tuna fish, a non-living survivor, or a non-lazy bum? I've smelled, with my own nose, different bouquets but the only type I've ever seen, with my own eyes, is the flowery variety, so why a "bouquet of flowers?"

Am I paranoid, or is there some secret of time only I can't intuit? Former movie mogul Samuel Goldwyn said, "I never make predictions, especially about the future," and the hoi polloi are constantly referring to "future plans" and "advance warning." This implies there are alternatives like past plans and a past future. The past is equally beguiling. Why do we specify "past experience" and "never before?" Aren't all experiences "past?" Why does "before" have to be added to "never?" Is there a hidden quantum dimension called the "never after" waiting to be unearthed by string theory? I worry when someone tells me the "honest truth," or gives me a "garden salad" to eat, or something "100 percent pure" to drink. Does that mean that if they only tell me the truth or ply me with a mere salad or a beverage that's only 99.99 percent pure then I'm in "serious danger?" Do I over exaggerate? Please R.S.V.P. so I can overcome my state of uneasy anxiety.

Also, aren't acronyms supposed to be used as a shortening technique? Don't people realize that when they talk about their PIN number, an ATM machine, a DMZ zone, the HIV virus and an ABM missile they are effectively saying "number number," "machine machine," "zone zone," "virus virus" and "missile missile," respectively?

Most pleonasms, however, are not so stylish or "arranged" and denote only poor form. "Could you repeat that again?" is an example of a commonly used pleonasm. A redundancy can be avoided by saying either, "Could you say that again?" or "Could you repeat that?" Don't say "each and every" when "every" suffices. And we certainly don't need the Nixon-ese "at this point in time" when "at this time" works. And better still, "now." Nor do you need to say "she is a woman who" when "she is" will do, or use "if and when" when only "if" is required.

Perhaps I'm just an unprogressive conservative who pines for the halcyon days when you didn't need to qualify that a gift was free, a victim innocent, a fact true, a record new, and scholarship academic. In the past, one didn't have to specify strictly private or natural grass. Then again, some pleonasms like "cash money" and "disposable garbage" have evolved into possible states of non-redundancy given the ubiquitous plastic and the current penchant for recycling. Some might say that in the past "heterosexual sex" was pleonastic, but not today. Unfortunately, a former pleonasm, "healthy tan," has actually mutated into an oxymoronic state in our ozone-depleted world.

So, who is to blame? As I live and breathe, I think I can pinpoint the party likely responsible for our modern orgy of redundancy. To paraphrase Zola, j'accuse *Raid Bug Repellant*. They unveiled the slogan "Raid kills bugs dead" in 1966. To keep pace with this linguistic overkill, other advertisements stressed products that were "new innovations," "more superior" and "very unique." McDonald's isn't content to sell billions of hamburgers but "billions and billions"; *Soft Soap Body Wash* doesn't merely make you "clean," you become "more than just clean" and don't think the pleonastic process only flows towards aggrandizement. Isn't a dot miniscule enough? Must we endure microdots?

N.B. Making a duplicate copy of this text in any shape or form without my express, intended permission and sanctioned authorization is totally and utterly allowed, and indeed more preferable than alternative options.

❧ REDUNDANCY PUZZLE

Many expressions in English could be considered redundant today, but the following pairs, where one word always precedes the other, are still in common use. Fill the blanks with the missing word(s) that complete the pleonasm.

MISSING WORD(S)

1 aid & _____

2 cease & _____

3 each & _____

4 far & _____

5 first & _____

6 highways & _____

7 hue & _____

8 intents & _____

9 kit & _____

10 lo & _____

11 nook & _____

12 null & _____

13 over & _____

14 part & _____

15 pick & _____

16 prim & _____

17 rack & _____

18 rant & _____

19 safe & _____

20 trials & _____

21 vim & _____

22 ways & _____

23 wild & _____

24 will & _____

ANSWERS: p. 147

Conclusion

ALTHOUGH THE INTENT OF *Wordplay: Arranged and Deranged Wit* is primarily to surprise, entertain and amuse the reader, I'd like to think that it highlights the importance of playing with language. *Wordplay* shows that there is often a grey line between what is intentional and unintentional in English language wordplay. Great minds, such as Shakespeare, have mined linguistic errors into deliberate classic jewels.

With regards to early childhood development, child psychologists Richard Ely and Alyssa McCabe wrote an article in the journal *First Language*, where they stated that their research found that children, in a fifteen-month period between the ages of five years, five months and six years, eight months, used language play in their utterances almost 25 percent of the time. Yet the importance of language play in general education is rarely a fixture, notwithstanding the benefit of its inclusion being heralded by many famous child psychologists as far back as Jean Piaget and Lev Vygotsky.

Au contraire, mes amis. According to linguist David Crystal, when children arrive in school, they receive an implicit or explicit message that language play is not conducive to proper education. Increasingly, however, many educators and linguists believe that manipulating language is in fact a conduit towards a better overall education and even superior reading skills. In his book *Language Play*, David Crystal states that "The reason I find language play such a plausible candidate [in literacy] is because it provides a bridge between the two domains of language structure and use, both of which have long been considered essential aspects of a child's linguistic development."

For those of us well out of our formative years, wordplay has different benefits. Cognitively, the elderly are constantly encouraged to keep their minds active, including partaking in wordplay that might actually help break up some of that mind-numbing plaque that plagues our brains as entropy takes its inevitable course. Companies such as Lumosity stress the benefits of wordplay in improving cognitive abilities. In connection with dementia, Dr. Yaakov Stern, a clinical psychologist at Columbia University in New York City, has found that the more connections, or synapses, you can develop between brain cells, the more resistant they are to the disease.

Socially, these wordplay activities, such as my daily Facebook word puzzle, bring people into contact with others and aid in establishing a rapport within a word nerd community. This improves quality of life and offers personal enjoyment that is both free and environmentally friendly. So try it. You'll like it.

On the deranged side, the wealth of vocabulary in English creates many hilarious situations where anyone can slip up, no matter how educated or erudite we may be. We all make mistakes occasionally and, rather than be embarrassed by them, we should regard them as an expression of the richness that our chaotically flexible language provides, largely because of its highly idiomatic nature. With English increasingly becoming the world's *lingua franca*, and particularly with the growth of English occurring in those speaking it as a second language, this mangling is all but inevitable. It should be seen as the price we must pay for the supremacy of English as a world language.

I will leave the last word to Adam Gopnik who, in an article in the *New Yorker*, affirms: "Wit and puns aren't just décor in the mind; they're essential signs that the mind knows it's on, recognizes its own software and can spot the bugs in its own program."

ANSWERS

PART I ❧ CHAPTER 1

Homonym puzzle — pp. 34–35

1–tick tic	11–gnus' news
2–mite might	12–hare hair
3–earn ern	13–lyin' lion
4–mussel muscle	14–lynx links
5–whale wail	15–cheetah cheater
6–towed toad	16–mare mère
7–sole soul	17–hoarse horse
8–dear deer	18–boar bore
9–doe dough	19–gorilla guerilla
10–moose mousse	

Double meaning puzzle — pp. 36–37

1–ace	11–cheers	21–date
2–ball	12–coach	22–draw
3–bear	13–coast	23–drawers
4–beat	14–conglomerate	24–entrance
5–bill	15–copper	25–eruption
6–blues	16–country	26–exploit
7–bluff	17–court	27–flat
8–canines	18–cuff	28–free
9–cardinal	19–dart	29–flush
10–cause	20–dash	40–kind

Cryptic homonym puzzle — pp. 37–38

1–run	11–punch	21–beef
2–yen	12–mine	22–iron
3–bar	13–lead	23–flounder
4–degree	14–misses	24–yellow
5–spar	15–stem	25–firing
6–pride	16–model	26–deposited
7–twig	17–hood	27–P/polish
8–bureau	18–spruce	28–minute
9–bank	19–mean	
10–egg	20–minor	

PART I ❧ CHAPTER 4

Split definitive animal puzzle — pp. 56–57

1–antelope	10–crowbar	19–pussyfoot
2–assailed	11–curtail	20–rambling
3–bearable	12–defendant	21–rather
4–beefed	13–emulate	22–ration
5–bulldozer	14–mandrake	23–rebellion
6–canapé	15–molestation	24–timeshare
7–catholic	16–octopus	25–vamoose
8–concur	17–Oxford	
9–cowled	18–pigeon	

PART I ❧ CHAPTER 5

Quasi-oxymoron puzzle — pp. 61–62

1–dead	8–offensive	15–war
2–Lies	9–stop	16–teacher
3–host	10–grief	17–shrimp
4–Fire	11–heavyweight	18–music
5–sex	12–Wide Shut	19–butt
6–lawyers	13–ugly	20–Short
7–intelligence	14–war	21–shorts

PART I ⅋ CHAPTER 7

Real acronym puzzle — pp. 72–73

1–away on leave

2–Brazil, Russia, India, China

3–computer-aided design and computer-aided manufacturing

4–disc-operating system

5–experimental prototype community of tomorrow

6–fouled (or f*****) up beyond all recognition

7–gay, urban professional + -pie

8–hazardous material

9–Ingvar Kamprad Elmtaryd Agunnaryd

10–Judge Advocate General

11–keep it simple stupid

12–light amplified stimulated electronic radiation

13–Mothers Against Drunk Driving

14–not in my backyard

15–obsessive-compulsive disorder

16–People for the Ethical Treatment of Animals

17–quasi-stellar object

18–radio detection and ranging

19–situation normal: all fouled (or f*****) up

20–thank God it's Friday

21–United Nations International Children's Emergency Fund

22–video cassette recorder

23–World Health Organization

24–extra-large

25–you only live once

26–zone improvement plan

PART I ⅋ CHAPTER 8

Riddle puzzle — pp. 81–83

1–your age	11–silence or a secret
2–cold	12–river
3–your name	13–ear of corn
4–newspaper	14–hole
5–garbage truck	15–rug
6–stamp	16–European
7–towel	17–watermelon
8–one is hard to get up; the other is hard to get down	18–tomorrow
	19–coffin
9–one's breath	20–charcoal
10–fire	21–dictionary

PART II ⅋ CHAPTER 5

Redundancy puzzle — pp. 139–140

1–abet	9–kaboodle	17–ruin
2–desist	10–behold	18–rave
3–every	11–cranny	19–sound
4–wide/away	12–void	20–tribulations
5–foremost	13–done with	21–vigor
6–byways	14–parcel	22–means
7–cry	15–choose	23–woolly
8–purposes	16–proper	24–testament

SELECT BIBLIOGRAPHY

Alter, Robert & Frank Kermode (editors). *The Literary Guide to the Bible*. Cambridge: Belknap, 1987.

Authorized King James Version of the Bible. New York: National Publishing, 1978.

Ayto, John. *A Century of New Words*. Oxford, UK: OUP, 2007.

Baldick, Chris. *The Concise Oxford Dictionary of Literary Terms*. Oxford, UK: OUP, 2001.

Barber, Katherine. *Six Words You Never Knew Had Something to Do With Pigs*. Don Mills: OUP, 2006.

Baum, Paul F. (translator). *Anglo-Saxon Riddles of the Exeter Book*. Durham: Duke University Press, 1963.

Benstock, Bernard. *Joyce-Again's Wake*. Seattle: WUP, 1965.

Bierce, Ambrose. *The Devil's Dictionary*. Garden City: Doubleday, 1911.

Brock, Suzanne. *Idiom's Delight*. New York: Vintage, 1988.

Burckhardt, Sigurd. *Shakespearean Meaning*. Princeton: Princeton University Press, 1968.

Cariou, Heather Summerhayes. *Sixty-Five Roses: A Sister's Memoir*. Toronto: McArthur, 2006.

Carroll, Lewis. *Through the Looking-Glass*. London, UK: Dent, 1954.

Coffin, Charles M. *The Complete Poetry & Selected Prose of John Donne*. New York: Modern Library, 2001.

Collins Complete Works of Oscar Wilde. Glasgow, Scotland: Harper Collins, 1999.

Cooper, Gloria (editor). *Red Tape Holds Up New Bridge*. New York: Perigree, 1987.

Cousineau, Phil. *Riddle Me This*. Berkeley: Conari, 1999.

Crystal, David. *Language Play*. London, UK: Penguin, 1988.

De Vries, Peter. *Without a Stitch in Time*. Chicago: UCP, 2014.

Dickens, Charles. *The Fireside Dickens*. London, UK: Chapman & Hall, 1903.

Farb, Peter. *Word Play: What Happens When People Talk*. New York: Vintage, 1963.

Franklin, Benjamin. *Poor Richard's Almanac*. Toronto: SN, 1918.

Fox, Christopher (editor). *The Cambridge Companion to Jonathan Swift*. Cambridge, UK: CUP, 2003.

Frazier, J.G. *The Golden Bough*. New York: Macmillan, 1963.

Grothe, Mardy. *Never Let a Fool Kiss You and Never Let a Kiss Fool You*. New York: Viking, 1999.

Hall, Max. *An Embarrassment of Misprints*. Golden: Fulcrum, 1995.

Hauptman, Don. *Cruel & Unusual Puns*. New York: Laurel, 1991.

Holy Scriptures. Tel-Aviv, Israel: Sinai Publishing, 1979.

Johnson, Samuel. *A Dictionary of the English Language*. London, UK: Offer, 1824.

Jay, Anthony (editor). *Oxford Dictionary of Political Quotations*. Oxford, UK: OUP, 2004.

Joseph, Sister Miriam. *Shakespeare's Use of the Arts of Language*. New York: Hafner, 1966.

Joyce, James. *Finnegans Wake*. London, UK: Faber & Faber, 1939.

Joyce, James. *Ulysses*. Mineola: Dover, 2002.

Kemp, Peter (editor). *Oxford Dictionary of Literary Quotations*. Oxford, UK: OUP, 2002.

Kingsolver, Barbara. *The Poisonwood Bible*. New York: Harper Flamingo, 1998.

Knowles, Elizabeth (editor). *Oxford Dictionary of Modern Quotations*. Oxford, UK: OUP, 2002.

Knowles, Elizabeth (editor). *Oxford Dictionary of Quotations*. Oxford, UK: OUP, 2004.

Lederer, Richard. *Anguished English*. Charleston: Wyrick, 1987.

Lederer, Richard. *Crazy English*. New York: Pocket, 1989.

Lederer, Richard. *Get Thee To a Punnery*. Charleston: Wyrick, 1988.

Lederer, Richard. *More Anguished English*. New York: Delacote, 1993.

Macrone, Michael. *Brush Up Your Shakespeare*. New York: Harper & Row, 1990.

Mahood, Molly. *Shakespeare's Wordplay*. London, UK: Methuen, 1957.

Martin, Robert Bernard. *The Triumph of Wit*. Oxford, UK: Clarendon, 1974.

McArthur, Tom (editor). *Concise Oxford Companion to the English Language*. Oxford, UK: OUP, 2005.

McCrum, Robert. *Globish: How the English Language Became The World's Language*. Toronto: Doubleday, 2010.

Opie, Ione & Peter. *The Lore and Language of Schoolchildren*. London, UK: OUP, 1967.

The Oxford English Dictionary Online. Oxford, UK: OUP, 2000.

Partridge, Eric. *The Shaggy Dog Story*. New York: Philosophical Library, 1954.

Peacham, Henry. *Peacham's Compleat Gentleman*. London, UK: Clarendon, 1906.

Pinker, Steven. *The Language Instinct: How the Mind Creates Language*. New York: Morrow, 1994.

Redfern, W.D. *Puns*. London, UK: Blackwell, 1984.

Rosten, Leo. *The New Joys of Yiddish*. New York: Crown, 2002.

Rowling, J.K. *Harry Potter & the Chamber of Secrets*. New York: Levine, 2004.

Rowling, J.K. *Harry Potter & the Philosopher's Stone*. London, UK: Bloomsbury, 1997.

Rubinstein, Frankie. *Dictionary of Shakespeare's Sexual Puns and Their Significance*. Hampshire, UK: Macmillan, 1989.

Sagarin, Edward. *The Anatomy of Dirty Words*. New York: Stuart, 1968.

Shakespeare, William. *The Complete Works of William Shakespeare*. New York: Books Inc., 1956.

Sheridan, Richard Brinsley. *The Rivals*. London, UK: Benn, 1979.

Sherrin, Ned (editor). *Oxford Dictionary of Humorous Quotations*. Oxford, UK: OUP, 2001.

Smollett, Tobias. *The Expedition of Humphry Clinker*. New York: Modern Library, 1929.

Spector, Robert D. *Smollett's Women*. Westport: Greenwood Press, 1994.

Spiegelman, David. *Medical Malaprops*. Van Nuys: Martin & Lawrence, 2005.

Styron, William. *Darkness Visible: a memoir of madness*. New York: Vintage, 1992.

Swainson, Bill (editor). *Encarta Book of Quotations*. New York: St. Martin's, 2000.

Symphosius. *The Hundred Riddles of Symphosius*. Woodstock: Elm Tree, 1912.

Taylor, Archer. *A Bibliography of Riddles*. Helsinki, Finland: Suomalainen Tiedeakatemia, 1939.

Tolkien, J.R.R. *The Hobbit*. Boston: Houghton Mifflin, 2002.

Truss, Lynne. *Eats Shoots & Leaves*. New York: Penguin, 2003.

Twain, Mark. *The Adventures of Huckleberry Finn*. New York: Harper, 1951.

Wallraff, Barbara. *Word Fugitives*. New York: Harper, 2006.

Wilson, C.P. *Jokes*. London, UK: Academic, 1979.

Wolfensten, Martha. *Children's Humor: A Psychological Analysis*. Glencoe: Free Press, 1954.

ABOUT THE AUTHOR

Howard Richler is a long-time logophile who has served as a language columnist for several newspapers and magazines. He is the author of seven previous books on language, including *The Dead Sea Scroll Palindromes* (1995), *Take My Words: A Wordaholic's Guide to the English Language* (1996), *A Bawdy Language: How a Second-Rate Language Slept its Way to the Top* (1999), *Global Mother Tongue: The Eight Flavours of English* (2006), *Can I Have a Word with You?* (2007), *Strange Bedfellows: The Private Lives of Words* (2010) and, most recently, *How Happy Became Homosexual and Other Mysterious Semantic Shifts* (2013). Richler resides with his partner Carol in Montreal, where he struggles to be fluent not only in French but in the many flavours of the English language. You can check out his language musings and daily word puzzles on Facebook at facebook.com/howard.richler and on Twitter @howardrichler. You can also visit his wordnerd blog at howarderichler.blogspot.com.

INDEX